The Silent Infodemic within South African Sign Language: Developing Human Language Technologies for South African Sign Language

Published by African Sun Media under the SUN PReSS imprint
Place of publication: Stellenbosch, South Africa

This publication was subjected to an independent double-blind peer evaluation by the publisher.

First edition 2026

ISBN 978-1-0671559-2-6
ISBN 978-1-0671559-3-3 (eBook)
https://doi.org/10.52779/9781067155933

Set in Times New Roman 10/13

Cover design, typesetting and production by African Sun Media
Cover image: © African Sun Media

SUN PReSS is an imprint of African Sun Media. Scholarly, professional and reference works are published under this imprint in print and electronic formats.

Our publications can be ordered from:
orders@africansunmedia.co.za
Takealot: bit.ly/2monsfl
Google Books: bit.ly/2k1Uilm
africansunmedia.store.it.si (eBooks)
Amazon: amzn.to/2ktL.pkL
JSTOR: https://bit.ly/3udc057

Visit africansunmedia.co.za for more information.

THE SILENT INFODEMIC

within South African Sign Language

Developing Human Language Technologies
for South African Sign Language

EDITOR: DR HERKULAAS MVE COMBRINK

SUN PRESS

CONTENTS

PREFACE

South African Sign Language (SASL) is more than a means of communication; it is a living expression of cultural identity, social history, and epistemic depth. Yet, for far too long, it has been overlooked, under-represented, and structurally excluded from the domains of technological development that increasingly shape public life. This book emerges from a deep conviction that the future of language technology must be inclusive, that the Deaf community must not only be present in the digital era, but must lead, shape, and define it. To do so, a critical mass of skills centred around human language technology for SASL needs to be established.

This work was written with urgency, but also with hope. It seeks to provide a roadmap for the development of SASL human language technologies and their related skills, grounded in community leadership, educational transformation, and research. Drawing on interdisciplinary scholarship, policy analysis, and computer and data science, it offers frameworks for building a future in which technological innovation lies at the heart of SASL Deaf communities.

This book is intended for a diverse readership, including researchers, technologists, educators, students, policymakers, and above all, Deaf professionals and advocates working to create space for SASL in the digital sphere. It does not present a finished solution, but rather a living invitationto rethink assumptions, redesign systems, and rebuild relationships between knowledge, power, and language.

"This book is one contribution to that journey."

Dr. HMvE Combrink, University of the Free State, 2025

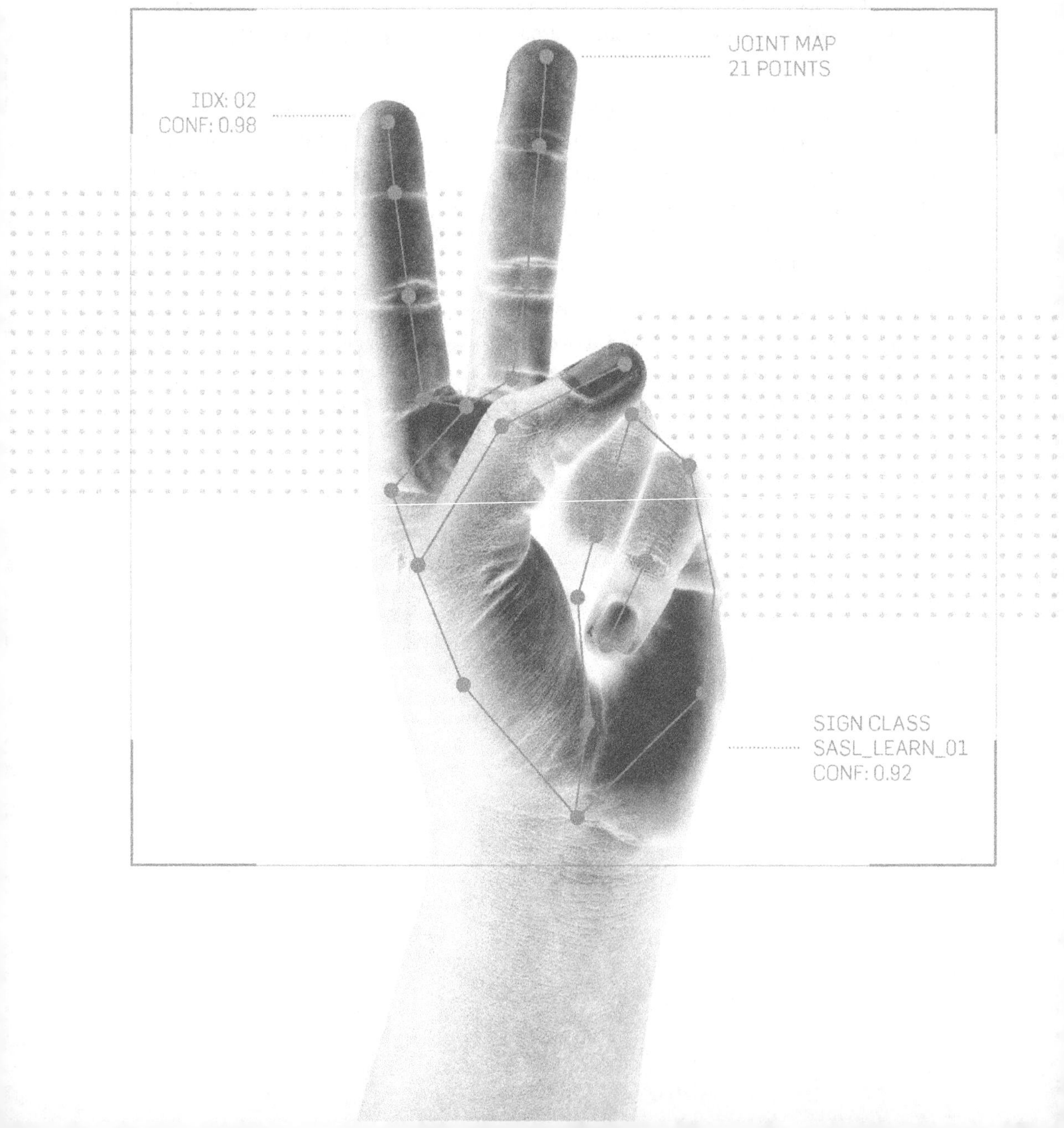
JOINT MAP
21 POINTS
IDX: 02
CONF: 0.98
SIGN CLASS
SASL_LEARN_01
CONF: 0.92

CHAPTER 1

The Silent Infodemic Among Deaf South Africans in Language Technology Development

Dr. Herkulaas Combrink and Mrs. Elizabeth Deysel

1.1 Introduction

The purpose of this book is to shed light on the language technology infodemic and provide a value-dependent account of language technologies for the South African Deaf community. In other words, the purpose of this book is to argue that the critical mass needed for developing language technologies, specifically for South African Sign Language (SASL), needs to be developed. In addition, Deaf communities should ultimately be involved in conceptualising, developing, and driving human language technologies for SASL, through a coherent research agenda that is inclusive of the needs of Deaf communities. At the heart of this book is the recognition that we are living through an infodemic, a term that typically refers to the rapid spread of misinformation and disinformation, especially in times of health-related crises, However, for the Deaf community, the infodemic takes on a more foundational form. It begins not with falsehoods, but with omissions caused by inherent hearing biases (Holcomb *et al.,* 2025). Hearing biases refer to a viewpoint that is skewed toward a hearing perspective and, in the context of this book, away from a Deaf standpoint on the matter (Leigh, 1999). The matter at hand then, is to develop human language technologies for the SASL Deaf communities.

An unintended consequence of having bias, is that the technology, and its use, would lack the required context tofully cater to all people it aims to serve - in this case, those who are Deaf, hard of hearing, or whose primary language is sign language (Wolf *et al.,* 2024). The silent infodemic refers to an epidemic of information voids, of systems that exclude signed languages from their design, of data infrastructures that overlook visual grammar, and of technologies that claim to be "accessible" while resting on assumptions rooted entirely in spoken, auditory, and hearing-centric norms. Hearing-centric norms refer to a perspective that is imposed by persons not involved in Deaf communities, nor having any practical knowledge of Deaf cultures, who nonetheless proceed to speak on behalf of Deaf communities without a proper mandate or engagement. We argue that technological advancement requires Deaf communities to be part of the research and development process, rather than mere users of it. This book exists to amplify what Deaf communities have long known, and long expressed, which is that language access is not a technical feature; it is a matter of dignity, identity, and power (De Meulder, 2016). While there exists some research in human language technology for SASL, it is not yet sufficient without a coherent research agenda.

We argue that the Deaf infodemic will not end with more apps, more policies, or more awareness campaigns alone. It will end when the value of signed languages is embedded in the very foundations of how we build, govern, and imagine technology - when Deaf and hard of hearing people are not afterthoughts in innovation, but architects of it. This can only be achieved through a coherent research focus, one where the problems, needs, and solutions to these problems are led through a research agenda that involves all relevant stakeholders as part of the research ecosystem. This ecosystem includes academic institutions, non-governmental organisations, governmental organisations, private industry and entrepreneurs. At present, those engaging in corpus development, human language technology research, algorithm design, and training data for SASL do so out of interest. However, compared to other South African languages, the resource distributions for human language technology development are not yet reflective of the scale these technologies require (Moape *et al.,* 2025). Let this book be both a mirror and a map, a reflection of where we are, and a direction for where we must go to advance human language technology for SASL.

1.2 SASL Human Language Technology Research

A lot of research in SASL human language technology centres around information and communication technologies in very specific domains, such as health, education, and technical fields (Magongwa, 2024; Haricharan *et al.,* 2017). One such example is the SignSupport initiative (Naranjo-Zeledón *et al.,* 2019). SignSupport hosts a collection of mobile applications as an innovative Deaf contact centre to support SASL, and the Deaf communities in South Africa (Blake *et al.,* 2014). In the context of SignSupport, a large emphasis is placed on healthcare-related interventions like Deaf Chat, a communication mediation-based platform between healthcare professionals and Deaf clients (Cooper *et al.,* 2023). SignSupport technologies involve Deaf interpreters and digital platforms (Tucker, 2015). An important part of the research on the platform is led by the National Institute for the Deaf (NID), Deaf Community of Cape Town (DCCT), and research teams within the University of the Western Cape (UWC). At the core of SignSupport is the emphasis on Deaf inclusion in the research, especially the design of the Deaf centred User Experience (UX) design of the platforms (Tovide *et al.,* 2022). The UWC Computer Science department, through the Bridging Applications and Networks Gaps (BANG) team, leads multi-partner research and app development initiatives addressing the everyday challenges of Deaf South Africans (Motlhabi *et al.,* 2013). This research team focuses on co-creation methodologies, bridging technical innovation and promoting social inclusion. The university's unique approach integrates UX research, backend automation (Salesforce & Zapier), and zero-rated mobile access, transforming medical, emergency, and educational communication systems for SASL users.

UWC is a central hub in the ecosystem, ensuring Deaf-centric design in public health and service delivery systems. Another research agenda within South Africa; is at the University of the Free State (UFS). Within the UFS, the core focus is on advancing human language technology for SASL by developing interoperable open-source tools and datasets (Combrink *et al.,* 2025). To do so, the UFS technological development includes the niche research field of SASL, centred on SASL place names, related Toponymy studies, social inclusion, and other SASL-related socio-linguistic research agendas (Siyavoshi & Sibanda, 2024; Loth *et al.,* 2021). The sociolinguistic niche is driven by the Department of SASL and Deaf Studies. At the UFS, the human language technology context focuses strongly on the creation of synthetic data for finger signing and sign language production tasks. The UFS research includes synthetic data generation using generative adversarial networks (GANs) to address the scarcity of annotated SASL data, supporting deep learning models in sign recognition and translation (Combrink *et al.,* 2025). GANs are deep learning algorithms sometimes used in artificial intelligence (AI) tools that generate synthetic data which closely emulates real data. Tools like LebitsoApp and the Deaf-oriented financial literacy initiative ("Good Money Habits") exemplify practical deployments. UFS promotes open data and community-driven development, ensuring ethical AI practices while empowering both linguistic and economic inclusion for the Deaf community.

While impressive that research teams are working on and addressing several challenges in research for human language technology advancements in SASL, the current research and community initiatives alone are not enough to cater to the needs of the South African Deaf community. Furthermore, SASL research in terms of fundamental human language technology advancement is not yet mature enough for benchmarks, problems that need addressing, and technological advancement to assist the Deaf community to be universally accepted research agendas. Part of this problem is that Deaf language technology development is the result of a select few researchers and individuals in human language technology who actively work on their research niche, as opposed to a universal SASL human language technology research agenda.

1.3 The Deaf Language Technology Infodemic

An infodemic is a crisis within a crisis, a silent storm of misinformation and missing information that may spread faster than the truth itself (Eysenbach, 2002). An infodemic arises when information voids dominate the landscape (Chiou *et al.,* 2022). These voids are not merely about having no data; they are the result of systemic exclusion, structural silences, and the absence of accessible, relevant information. Information voids are typically laden with uncertainty, where the truth is contested, even among experts. To illustrate this, the COVID-19 vaccine rollout had an abundance of information voids, which led to misinformation among other challenges (Ouyang *et al.,* 2022).

To a lesser extent, when the first COVID-19 vaccine was released to the public, truths, speculations, and basic understandings of vaccines were debated despite vaccine science being an old construct (Chen *et al.,* 2022). Even though mRNA vaccines were commonly known scientifically among vaccine scientists and medical scientists, the mRNA COVID-19 vaccines were deeply contested because they were not commonly known by the public (Teodoro *et al.,* 2021). When information doesn't reach everyone equally, people are left to fill the gaps themselves, often with assumptions, myths, or incorrect second-hand knowledge (Fricker, 2006). Infodemics that have consequences to public health outcomes need to be managed because, if they are not, they alter social behaviourand reduce health-seeking behaviours. This in turn perpetuates poor health outcomes due to fear, uncertainty, and other factors, including misinformation (Do Nascimento *et al.,* 2022).

Infodemics have been described since 2002 due to the abundant misinformation around the Middle Eastern Respiratory Syndrome (MERS), a type of coronavirus (Eysenbach, 2002). As described, the MERS infodemic led to an abundance of uncertainty, and poor public outcomes for the populations that were affected by it, and yet, sanctions were put in place to contain MERS to the Middle East. Since then, several authors have written about studies related to infodemics to understand how misinformation, disinformation, conspiracy theories, and other forms of misinformed knowledge about concepts impacting health have been disseminated (Adebesin *et al.,* 2023; Chowdhury *et al.,* 2023; Pool *et al.,* 2021). Indeed, infodemics are primarily studied and managed in health, in particular public health, but we argue that infodemics are present across all domains of knowledge where there is uncertainty.

In the South African context, the Deaf population faces a silent infodemic, not due to a lack of intelligence or curiosity, but because the systems designed to inform and include have overlooked them at every technological and institutional level. The specific infodemic of misinformed beliefs around the Deaf stems from assumptions about Deaf cultures, signed language, and hearing contexts within deep information voids about the true nature of these concepts. The primary technological infodemic within Deaf digital communication technologies is caused by innovations created by hearing individuals without Deaf context, appropriation, or knowledge. This creates a profound disconnect between the tools we build and the people who need them.

1.4 The Fallacy of Speech-to-Text as a Viable Solution for Deaf Communities

One of the most glaring examples of the Deaf language technology infodemic lies in the dominance of speech-to-text technologies in hearing spaces, which are often championed as accessibility solutions for Deaf communities (Millett, 2021). Speech-to-text technologies were not originally conceptualised or designed to serve Deaf communities, but rather as a solution for dictation and spoken translation tasks. While speech-to-text might be beneficial in some contexts, it is fundamentally a hearing-centric solution (Miller, 2024).

The contexts in which speech-to-text is necessary relate to situations where dialogue-based conversations (team meetings), public speeches (news), accountability measures associated with talking (parliament), legal vetting (courtrooms), and other forms of instruction and/

or information need to be captured from people who use speech as their primary form of communication. Speech-to-text has an important place in society, and as a human language technology, however it assumes that spoken language is the primary mode of communication and comprehension for all people and contexts, which it is not. Speech-to-text technology also assumes that literacy is adequate for everyone to understand the textand the jargon, and that they can read at an adequate rate to compensate for the text being produced (Maryadi *et al.,* 2022).

For speech-to-text to work, it assumes that all people reading the text are proficient in the syntax and grammar of the speech-to-text language output (Gramkow, 2023). For speech-to-text to also be fully effective, there is an underlying assumption that everyone understands the dialogue and the purpose of the dialogue (Berke *et al.,* 2018). None of these assumptions are universal truths for any Deaf community (Coy, 2022). It ignores the fact that for many Deaf South Africans, SASL is the first and most fluent language (Kelly *et al.,* 2022; Andrade & Baloyi, 2011). Why is there such an abundance of speech-to-text innovation, and yet a glaring absence of speech-to-sign solutions? Why are we still waiting for sign language recognition systems when AI can already write poetry, generate hyper-realistic images, and translate dozens of spoken languages in real time?

The answer lies in a combination of things, including a lack of prioritisation and investment, the complexity of the solutions, the available skills and knowledge to drive innovation, as well as broader technological buy-in to create adequate resources, such as reliable SASL training data to innovate such technologies. Sign recognition technology remains in its infancy globally, but in South Africa, it is nearly non-existent. The digital silence around SASL reflects a deeper social silence, one that denies Deaf individuals the opportunity to see their language flourish in modern digital spaces.

At first glance, speech-to-text technology is often classified as an inclusive, modern solution for Deaf accessibility (Freitas, 2010). But this perception is deeply flawed for all Deaf communities, and in many ways, dangerously misleading. First, it is critical to understand that spoken languages and signed languages are fundamentally different in structure, expression, and cognitive processing (Talmy, 2003). Spoken languages have sound, structure, symbols, and entire lexical systems. Spoken languages have also been formalised as communication systems for centuries. Spoken languages thus have a more developed way in which language acquisition is transferred. For example, the acquisition of words stems from letters, and these letters stem from sounds matched to symbols. If you remove this foundational building block from language acquisition and replace it with signed language acquisition, like SASL acquisition, then the modality of communication fundamentally changes. SASL is a complete, natural language with its own syntax, grammar, and rules that are visually and spatially expressed, not written, and certainly not tied to spoken language phonetics (Prinsloo, 2003). It is a linguistic system that exists in three dimensions involving space, movement, and facial expression. By contrast, speech-to-text tools are built on spoken language rules and sound-based sequencing, a foundation that has no linguistic equivalence in SASL.

What makes this even more problematic is the assumption that Deaf individuals are simply 'hearing people who can't hear' and, therefore, that text-based content is universally effective (Desselle & Proctor, 2000). This assumption is truly misinformed by hearing people who often share this belief in the absence of relevant information. Again, this type of misinformation erases the reality that many Deaf individuals acquire signed language as their first language, while spoken and written language may come much later, if at all, depending on access to quality education. This delay in language exposure, known as language deprivation, means that many Deaf individuals are not native readers or writers of the dominant spoken language in their region. Therefore, speech-to-text is not simply a matter of providing 'the words' and expecting there to be meaning by providing text. When text is presented to the average Deaf person, it is full of unfamiliar syntax, grammar, and idioms that often have no intuitive connection to the person's first language, a signed language.

Further compounding the issue is how academic and policy literature often echoes this fallacy, framing speech-to-text as a catch-all fix for Deaf accessibility. In doing so, it elevates a hearing-centric solution as universally valid, while pushing aside the lived realities and preferences of Deaf individuals themselves. Academic experts on Deaf culture sometimes run the risk of conducting research that might have a logical 'cause-effect-solution' to a Deaf-centred problem, but from a hearing perspective. This, in turn, risks reinforcing inaccurate academic literature, leading to inaccurate innovations that ultimately reflect a hearing perspective - an unintended consequence of the bias initially introduced in the research to begin with.

Another major scope of misinformation is the matter of literacy among the Deaf and hard-of-hearing communities. South Africa already struggles with significant literacy challenges across the population (Mojapelo, 2023). In several studies, it was shown that South African literacy is among the lowest globally in public schools, and this is specific to hearing schools (Mogofe & Athiemoolam, 2025; Taylor & Mawoyo, 2022; Meiklejohn *et al.,* 2021; Southwood *et al.,* 2021). When Deaf and hard-of-hearing schools are considered, Deaf learners are disproportionately affected due to systemic barriers in early education, lack of exposure to bilingual education (SASL and written language), and minimal access to reading materials in accessible formats (Akach, 2010). To then present rapid, unedited, real-time text, as most speech-to-text systems do, is just simply an ineffective method of communication. Speech-to-text also ignores how cognitively demanding and exclusionary speed reading can be if a person solely relies on the rapid text generation platforms to follow a dialogue in real-time. For Deaf individuals with limited reading fluency in English or other spoken languages, this stream of rapid-fire text becomes a wall of noise, different from sound, but just as impenetrable. How can a dialogue between two hearing people be followed by a Deaf person with only moderate text literacy?

Imagine being in a scenario where two people speak a language you do not understand, and in order to follow the conversation, you are forced to look at a screen, without having any tonality cues. This task will be both exhausting and illegible for most hearing people with proper training. The barrier to understanding is simply too large and marginalising.

When Deaf users rely on these flawed outputs to make critical decisions, for example, in school, at work, in hospitals, or during national broadcasts, the cost is not just confusion, but misinformed decisions that can impact health, safety, education, dignity, and more importantly, basic understanding.

The real tragedy is that hearing professionals in software development, academic research, and policymaking, are often unaware that speech-to-text is not truly an enabling innovation, but in fact, a lazy substitution for real inclusion. Instead of investing in Deaf-centred technologies, like real-time speech-to-sign systems or AI-driven SASL avatars, the industry continues to pour resources into tools that force Deaf people to navigate a world not designed for them. Technologies that are widely adopted by the Deaf are not speech-to-text-based tools, but rather technologies that have utility and usability to the communities themselves, and which promote inclusion and connection. When tools developed for the Deaf do not serve a valid fit for purpose, the Deaf community voices their dissatisfaction or critiques, but their feedback is too often ignored, marginalised, and not taken seriously because a real solution might not yet exist or be difficult to implement.

This is not just a technical issue. It is a question of epistemic injustice: whose language is seen as valid, whose communication is prioritised, and who gets to define what "access" looks like. As long as speech-to-text is treated as the default accessibility tool, the core fallacy will continue with the idea that Deaf people must be linguistically flexible, while hearing systems remain rigid.

True accessibility cannot be built on flawed assumptions. It must begin with an honest understanding that access is not just about content delivery, but language, cultural relevance, and dignity. Speech-to-text, in its current state, is not a bridge. For many Deaf people, it is a wall, a true barrier, and not a technology that can be used. Speech-to-text technologies require hearing people, not Deaf people, and if a hearing person is not present, then the tool cannot be used. This is not inclusion; this is the purest form of marginalisation. One of the best ways governments, policy makers, investors, and creators, including entrepreneurs, can increase accessibility is by allocating resources that can address this problem; currently those resources are insufficient.

1.5 A Lack of Resource Infodemic

Beyond technological neglect, there is also a major shortage of resources for the Deaf (Moape *et al.*, 2025). A lack of resources for a specific community promotes isolation, separation, and societal exclusion (Silver, 2007). One such example is the much-contested Eurocentric infiltration of toys into the African market (Gutierrez, 2017). All dolls at some point in time were white dolls, with blonde hair and blue eyes, none of which truly reflected all local African contexts. This subtle cultural artifact had profound consequences related to identity, beauty, and the associated standards, introducing bias into different cultural contexts (Stam & Shohat, 1994). Much like this type of superimposed bias, the hearing superimposes stories, books, and literature that do not cater to the Deaf (Morgan, 2008). This excludes a body of literature authored by Deaf individuals or written in a way that centres

Deaf experiences. Deaf children grow up with very few stories in their own language. Their cultural identity, history, and everyday realities are under-represented in media, education, and research. The ecosystem of Deaf language development, storytelling, and content creation is fragile and underdeveloped, making it incredibly difficult to challenge stereotypes or to educate the hearing world about Deaf perspectives.

This shortage is not a coincidence; it is the direct consequence of years of institutional exclusion, policy neglect, and societal indifference toward Deaf narratives and knowledge systems (Holness, 2016). From childhood, Deaf individuals are often raised in environments where their primary language, a signed language, is barely present, if at all (Kyle *et al.,* 1988). For many, their early experiences with education, storytelling, media, and social engagement are filtered through the lens of spoken language, a system that is not their own. As a result, Deaf children grow up with limited access to books, digital content, or curriculum that reflects their language, culture, or reality (Lederberg *et al.,* 2013). The formative power of stories, those that help children see themselves in the world, build confidence, shape identity, and connect to a community, is denied to them. If this denial leaves hearing people with creativity deficits, can you imagine the impact on an already marginalised Deaf child? When stories in your language don't exist, it doesn't just silence your voice; it calls into question whether your voice even matters.

In a country with 12 official spoken languages, including the recent addition of SASL, resource allocation remains unequal. Deaf language access is not yet truly national, nor is it fully integrated. The problem is that when there are no platforms, no data frameworks, and no policies that prioritise Deaf inclusion, then the information void becomes a breeding ground for a harmful infodemic, one that strips Deaf individuals of their agency, their voice, and their rightful seat at the table.

There is a strikingly limited body of literature authored by Deaf individuals in South Africa, with even works written with Deaf audiences in mind. Most available content is filtered througha hearing gaze: academic studies about Deaf people, charity messaging that paints Deafness as a deficit, or educational material that treats SASL as an add-on instead of a foundation. True Deaf authorship, narratives that are not translated but created in SASL or bilingually, remains vanishingly rare, not because Deaf people lack creativity or insight, but because the ecosystem needed to nurture and publish such work has been starved of investment, visibility, and support.

The exclusion of the appropriate Deaf literature and cultural artifacts extends far beyond books. In the media, SASL is seldom featured, unless reduced to a small, interpreted window in a corner of the screen, symbolically included, yet practically sidelined. Mainstream television, radio, and digital platforms still fail to incorporate Deaf creators or SASL-native content into their programming. Deaf characters in film and TV are often written by hearing people, portrayed by hearing actors, and built around hearing interpretations of Deaf experience. An unintended consequence of this exclusion of the Deaf communities leaves the public with a skewed, often patronising view of Deaf lives, while Deaf audiences are forced to consume content that does not reflect their reality.

In education, the absence of SASL-first content means that many Deaf learners must try to learn abstract concepts in a second or third language, often without adequate interpretation. In an education system where there is a major need to innovate opportunities to improve language outcomes and increase educational material in "native" South African languages, why are Deaf learners not part of the upliftment? Being Deaf is not a choice for many, and most Deaf children are born into hearing homes. Exclusion not only deepens educational inequality but also restricts intellectual development and compounds social isolation. In research, Deaf voices are under-represented or excluded entirely, treated as subjects to be studied, rather than as co-researchers or authors of their own epistemologies.

The cultural invisibility of Deaf stories, literature, and lived experiences has long-term consequences. Without platforms that elevate Deaf voices, without stories that "humanise" Deaf experiences, without data frameworks that preserve SASL as a legitimate and living language, stereotypes flourish. Hearing people continue to make assumptions about Deaf intelligence, ability, and potential. Misinformation continually spreads. Harmful narratives persist in entrenching distorted societal norms about the Deaf. The Deaf community comes to be seen not as a vibrant linguistic and cultural minority, but as a medical condition to be treated, a social burden to be carried, or an afterthought in diversity conversations.

In South Africa, SASL was only recognised in 2023, a symbolic victory, but one that has yet to translate into concrete, systemic inclusion (Carne *et al.,* 2024). While other languages benefit from broadcasting rights, curriculum development, translation services, and public funding, SASL continues to be treated as peripheral. It has not been integrated into national data infrastructures, government service design, or digital innovation agendas. There is no sufficient national SASL media fund, no universal strategic plan to elevate Deaf cultural production, and very little mainstream frameworks to ensure Deaf representation in the knowledge economy. Deaf resources require more input than text to become inclusive, and the funds to mobilise this much-needed upliftment, empowerment, and inclusion are just not invested.

Without policy that treats SASL as equal, without platforms designed with Deaf creators and consumers in mind, and without resource allocation that matches the scale of exclusion, Deaf communities will continue to live within a digital, educational, and cultural information void. These voids are not neutral; they are fertile ground for the infodemic to grow. When Deaf people are not seen, not understood, and not empowered to shape the information landscape in their own language, they are stripped of agency, authorship, and autonomy.

The exclusion of Deaf experts in language technology is not merely about what is missing; it is about what is being deliberately left out, even as the rest of society races into an AI-driven, data-rich, content-saturated future. Deaf people are being asked to participate in a world that refuses to provide them with the tools to do so. It is a denial of both equity and imagination. Because what would our media, education, and national story look like if Deaf perspectives were not only included, but centred? What myths could be broken? What innovations could be born?

Until we answer these questions with bold investment and authentic inclusion, the Deaf community will remain marginalised - not by silence itself, but by the systems that keep it in place.

1.6 Limited Training Data for Machine Learning (ML) and Artificial Intelligence (AI)

Data is the fuel of innovation (Trabucchi & Buganza, 2019). Without it, no technology can evolve (Lou, 2022). For the Deaf community, however, data scarcity has become a barrier, one that stifles innovation before it even begins. The irony is stark: we live in an age of Big Data, yet when it comes to SASL, the datasets are not just small, they are nearly non-existent. In machine learning, which forms a part of the AI ecosystem, there are supervised and unsupervised learning approaches (Alloghani *et al.,* 2020). Supervised learning is a set of algorithms that learn from pre-existing data to perform a specific task.

These tasks include classifying new datasets, grouping information, predicting new information, and generating synthetic data. In the context of language technology, the AI ecosystem has given rise to widely adopted systems that incorporate different types of methods, such as large language models (LLMs), to generate content and automate routine tasks, as seen in multi-agent systems (Li *et al.,* 2024). For language technology, text can now be translated to different languages, content can be created, and text can be widely analysed using these technologies. A fundamental underpinning for understanding these technologies resides in the data used to train these models, and for SASL, a lack of data directly translates to a lack of AI-driven innovation.

These datasets don't exist in a vacuum; they are cultivated over time through infrastructure, funding, community involvement, and a genuine commitment to inclusion. In the case of SASL, the foundational data needed to train recognition models, generate translations, or build assistive AI simply isn't there. There are no comprehensive sign corpora, no large-scale annotated video datasets, and limited linguistic resources for ML systems to learn from at present. Part of this specific problem is that there are limited national frameworks for data sharing, no centralised repositories of SASL media, and no consistent investment in capturing the richness of the language across regions and dialects. Most of the information that does exist is fragmented, scattered across academic projects, NGOs, or informal channels. This kind of fractured data environment makes it nearly impossible to develop reliable, inclusive technology that reflects the full range of SASL usage and culture.

Furthermore, data collection involving the Deaf community must be done ethically and inclusively, with Deaf people leading the process, not just appearing in front of a camera (Combrink *et al.,* 2025). The problem is that collecting SASL, or any other signed language data, requires a face, hands, and emotion. Given the strict policies for data collection, it is thus deemed the most sensitive data type to collect. If Deaf people are not at the of the SASL data economy - either as data scientists, linguistic consultants, or technical leaders - then the risk of creating tools that misrepresent, flatten, or even erase Deaf identity becomes high, as outlined earlier.

1.7 Gaps in the Deaf communities

Access to education, particularly in STEM fields like data science, ML, or software development, is not equitably available to Deaf learners in South Africa. This isn't just a question of access to classrooms, but of access to meaningful participation. There are organisations that promote data science skills for Deaf learners, but unfortunately, there is a lack in the data engineering and broader software development ecosystem to create truly novel, tailored applications for the South African Deaf communities - by the communities themselves. A further complication is that this ecosystem of development comprises not only the technical skills to develop software and manage data, but also the communication capabilities, ethical and philosophical rigour that requires data-driven AI software development. Without SASL interpreters trained in technical vocabulary, without curriculum materials adapted for Deaf students, and without mentors or role models who have walked that path, the pipeline from Deaf learner to tech innovator is almost non-existent.

While universities and tech hubs across the country are investing in Fourth Industrial Revolution (4IR) skills, the Deaf community is left behind. The Deaf community does not lack the potential, but the structures meant to empower are not designed to include. Deaf students often face interrupted education, particularly during the transition from secondary school to tertiary institutions. The leap is not only academic but also linguistic and cultural. A Deaf student in a university might be the only Deaf person in the room, learning in their second or third language, without any academic support that reflects their lived experience or communication style.

This lack of opportunity means that Deaf communities are under-represented not only as consumers of technology but also as creators, researchers, and leaders. Their absence from the innovation decision making process results in tools that are incomplete at best and exclusionary at worst. South Africa cannot solve the challenges of Deaf inclusion in tech without building inclusive tech talent pipelines, and that starts with investing in Deaf education, Deaf mentorship, and Deaf-led research. A possible tech pipeline can include placing semi-skilled Deaf technicians in research teams through internships to assist with human language technology design and development. For this to become a reality, resources must be put in place for interpreters, more SASL signers need to be included in language technology research teams, and professional SASL should be taught to all research team members who are a part of the human language technology team. Part of the agenda is to promote technological inclusion so that all innovation in SASL human language technology is Deaf-centred and conducted by all members of society driven towards this specific research agenda. At the core of this agenda, then, is driving solutions that have value and add impact.

What is important to understand is that the Deaf ecosystem in South Africa is not broken but rather that it is under-supported, underfunded, and structurally marginalised. SASL is rich in culture, identity, and innovation, but these strengths are constantly stifled by a lack of institutional backing. An infodemic thrives in silence, but the silence around Deaf inclusion in tech is not natural. It is a choice.

CHAPTER 2

Scoping AI and SASL Academic Research

Dr. Herkulaas Combrink, Dr. Sarah Siyavoshi,
Dr. Patric Sibanda, and Dr. Chrismi-Rinda Loth

2.1 Introduction

This chapter outlines a scoping review that presents the main findings regarding thematic trends and research gaps in interdisciplinary human language technology domains and discusses the implications for future interdisciplinary work at the intersection of South African Sign Language (SASL), Deaf Studies, Linguistics, and artificial intelligence (AI). In doing so, it establishes a foundation for understanding the current academic approaches to SASL and AI, and frames the need for more inclusive, ethical, and linguistically grounded data science research moving forward. The integration of AI into the study of SASL has introduced new research opportunities while exposing significant gaps in academic scholarship. With the recognition of SASL as one of South Africa's twelve official languages, there is a growing need to understand how AI, in all its guises - including machine learning technologies - is being applied within Deaf studies and sign linguistics (Reagan, 2020). However, despite increasing public attention, academic literature remains limited, fragmented, and largely focused on narrow technological applications.

By systematically surveying the available literature, the scoping review aims to offer a comprehensive overview of how the academic community has engaged with technological challenges in the development and application of AI for SASL.

2.2 Scoping Review

A scoping review is a systematic, exploratory research method that aims to map the existing body of knowledge on a specific topic, providing an overview of the breadth, depth, and nature of available evidence (Munn *et al.,* 2018). Unlike systematic reviews, which focus on narrowly defined questions often linked to specific outcomes, scoping reviews are designed to examine broader topics, to clarify key concepts, to identify main sources and types of evidence, and to uncover knowledge gaps within a research field (Mak & Thomas, 2022). Scoping reviews are particularly well suited to emerging, complex, or heterogeneous areas of inquiry where the literature is varied in approach, content, or quality (Barcelona *et al.,* 2024). The primary objective of a scoping review is to synthesise a wide range of information, offering insights into how a particular research domain is structured without necessarily assessing the methodological quality of individual studies (Tricco *et al.,* 2016).

Scoping reviews are therefore invaluable when mapping research landscapes, especially in fields where rapid technological advances, interdisciplinary convergence, or evolving social needs make comprehensive understanding critical (Dreksler *et al.,* 2025; Kain *et al.,* 2024; Murphy *et al.,* 2021). Typically, a scoping review follows a several stages, which start by formulating a clearly articulated review objective and set of questions. Thereafter, a scoping review focuses on developing and executing a comprehensive search strategy across relevant academic and grey literature sources. Once completed, rigorous inclusion and exclusion criteria are applied to select eligible studies, systematically charting or extracting relevant data, and finally, synthesising the findings in a manner that highlights overarching themes, trends, and research deficits (Pollock *et al.,* 2022).

Transparency and reproducibility are important, with detailed reporting often following recognised guidelines such as the Preferred Reporting Items for Systematic Reviews and Meta-Analyses extension for Scoping Reviews framework (PRISMA-ScR). Such frameworks ensure that a systemic approach is taken by those who conduct the scoping review so that the results may be repeated (Mattos *et al.,* 2023). Thus, within the context of this chapter, the scoping review serves not merely as a literature summary, but as a strategic, methodological foundation for scoping relevant literature within this domain.

2.3 Scoping Review Criteria

For this specific scoping review, the process was informed by PRISMA-ScR (Tricco *et al.,* 2018). The objective of the examination was to identify how AI has been engaged within SASL studies, based on academic literature; to evaluate the incorporation of linguistic, cultural, and community-driven concerns into technological research; and to chart existing gaps, ethical challenges, and interdisciplinary needs that could guide future work. Following the establishment of objectives, an extensive search strategy was devised. Four major academic databases were selected for the scoping review, namely Scopus, ProQuest One Academic, EBSCOhost, and Web of Science.

The choice of these academic databases was justified on the basis of their accreditation from the South African Department of Higher Education and Training (DHET), as well as reputable academic databases for scientific research. The search strategy used Boolean keyword combinations: "South African Sign Language" AND/OR "Machine Learning," "SASL" AND/OR "Artificial Intelligence"; "Sign Language Recognition" AND/OR "South Africa"; and "Deaf Community" AND/OR "Technology" AND/OR "South Africa." The search was intentionally broad in terms of publication date to capture the full extent of the research within these intersections. Next, the systematic application of inclusion and exclusion criteria to refine the dataset was adapted for SASL according to (Weerakkody & Rajapaksha, 2023).

Duplicate entries across databases were identified and meticulously removed, resulting in a refined pool of 1,847 unique records. Title and abstract screening followed, during which records were excluded if they failed to mention SASL specifically, addressed sign languages other than SASL without clear contextual relevance, or lacked an AI or ML component. General discussions of accessibility technologies unlinked to linguistic study, or metaphorical uses of sign language, were also excluded. Studies that passed this screening moved on to full-text review, during which the abstracts of 469 articles were examined. Articles were excluded at this stage for thematic misalignment, insufficient methodological rigour, non-peer-reviewed status, or irrelevance to the technological-linguistic focus of the review according to an adaptation of exclusion by Selçuk, (2019). The framework proposed by Selçuk, (2019) is to review the extracted literature and determine relevance on the basis of assessing the abstracts, titles, and/or keywords, depending on the depth of the analysis. This rigorous filtration process ultimately yielded a final corpus of six peer-reviewed academic articles all scoping criteria (Figure 2.1).

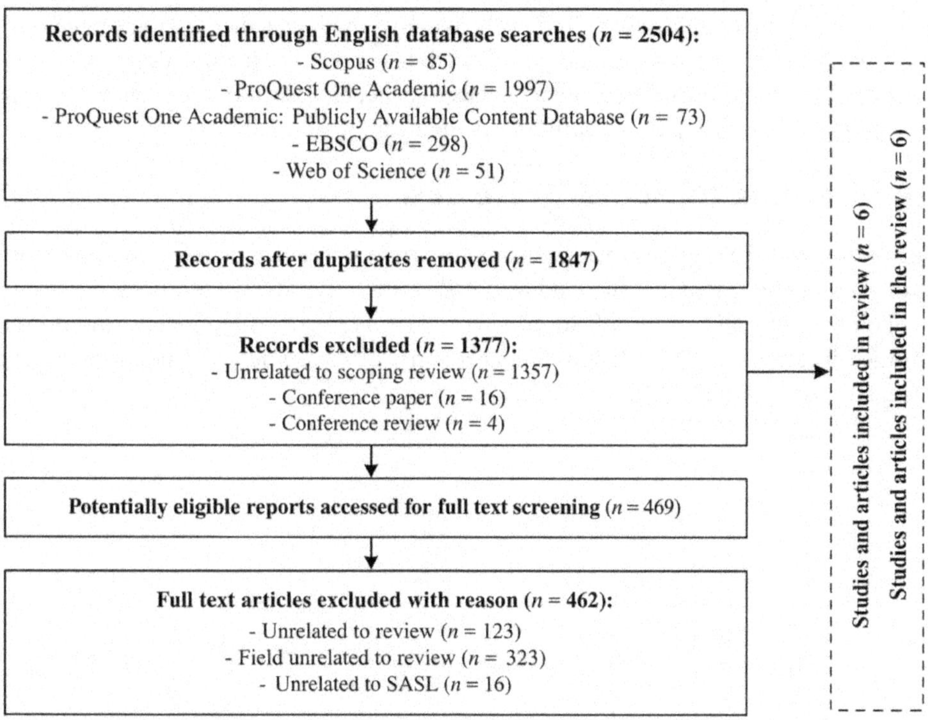

***Figure 2.1**: Scoping review criteria and filtering.*

With the final selection of articles in hand, a detailed data charting and extraction process was undertaken according to an adaptation of the approach used by Kuštelega *et al.*, (2025). According to Kuštelega *et al.*, (2025), in a study that examined several reports and articles, only the relevant articles and insights within the articles/reports in the scoping review were used. Similarly, our focus was on extracting specific information based on the inclusion criteria. For each study, metadata such as bibliographic information were recorded, including the title, authorship, year of publication, and source. In addition, the focus and objectives of the research were categorised, distinguishing between studies centred on AI, which included machine translation, recognition systems, or broader linguistic modelling. Methodological approaches were analysed, with particular attention paid to the type of AI and ML models used, characteristics of datasets used, and annotation strategies implemented. The degree of Deaf community engagement, that is, where the work actively involved that of a Deaf community as active researchers, was also documented where applicable, but with the core focus on the computational interdisciplinarity of the work, noting instances of participatory design, consultation, or respondent validation. Ethical considerations were systematically extracted, highlighting whether studies addressed issues of bias mitigation, data governance, community consent, and/or cultural sensitivity. The synthesis and presentation of results proceeded through thematic aggregation, rather than isolated study-by-study summaries. Emphasis was placed on identifying overarching trends within the studies. Particular attention was paid to discrepancies between technological advancements and linguistic or cultural safeguards, providing a nuanced understanding of where the field stands and where it urgently needs to evolve. The methodology ensured that the review's findings are not anecdotal or selective, but represent a structured, transparent, and comprehensive engagement with the available body of knowledge.

2.4 Findings of Scoping Review

One of the most striking observations emerging from the review is the dramatic surge in media and public discourse surrounding SASL in the year 2023. Following the historic recognition of SASL as one of South Africa's twelve official languages, there was a recorded increase of 1 210.89% in media reports, news articles, and popular coverage related to SASL (Figure 2.2).

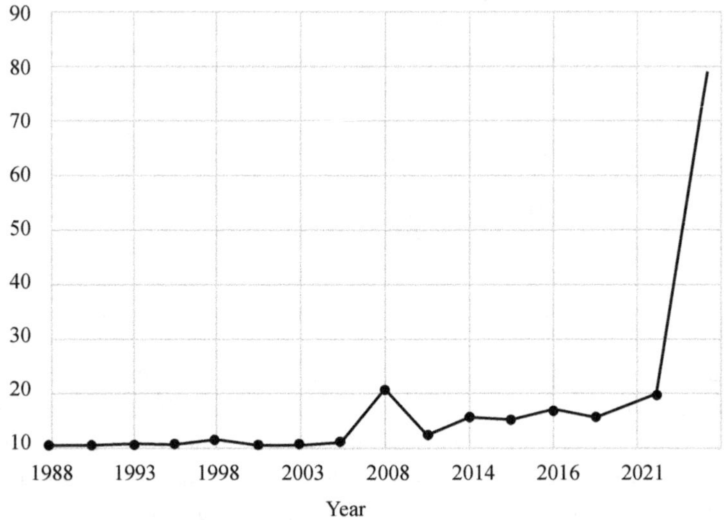

***Figure 2.2**: Global articles, news, and media releases related to SASL (n = 2504).*

This unprecedented spike indicates an intensified societal awareness and an increased demand for the development of SASL resources across education, governance, public services, and technology. However, when turning specifically to the realm of peer-reviewed academic scholarship at the intersection of ML and SASL, the review reveals a far more modest reality. Out of an initial pool of academic records, only six (n = 6) articles met the rigorous inclusion criteria set for this review. This outcome contrasts the surge in media attention, highlighting a critical lag between public interest and scholarly output in this field. A deeper analysis of the included articles shows that the majority of the research efforts are technologically oriented, with limited engagement in sociolinguistic or cultural dimensions integrated in the AI-related research. This indicates that the interdisciplinarity does not include a sociolinguistic contribution (Table 2.1).

Table 2.1: Summary of outlined articles

Core theme of article	Description
Sign Language Recognition Systems	Discusses the role of sign language in communication, the challenges in implementing recognition systems, and the potential of ML and artificial neural network models in improving accuracy levels for recognising sign language gestures.
Mobile Application for Sign Language Recognition	Explores the design and implementation of a mobile application for SASL recognition that connects to an instrumented glove via Bluetooth. The application uses different neural networks and a Support Vector Machine (SVM) for recognition.
Machine Translation from Spoken to Signed Languages	Addresses the challenges in translating from spoken languages to visual-spatial languages like SASL. The paper discusses the design and implementation of a preprocessor that uses areas of linguistics, such as anaphora resolution and a data structure called a scene graph, to help with the spatial aspect of the translation.
Prototype Machine Translation System	Presents a prototype machine translation system designed to translate English text into a gloss-based representation of SASL. The system uses a transfer-based approach and a tree adjoining grammar formalism.
Generic Avatar Animator for Sign Language Projects	Describes the design of a generic avatar animator for use in sign language projects. The animator can animate any avatar that is compliant with the H-Anim standard for humanoid animation.
Improving Multilingualism in Education with AI	Makes a case for employing AI to improve multilingualism in South Africa's education system. The article discusses the value of first-language education and how AI can be leveraged to facilitate education in all South African languages.

Of the six studies, most focused on either machine translation systems or recognition technologies. These works largely aimed to develop computational models capable of translating SASL signs into text or speech or recognising signs from video inputs. Their technological focus, while important, often lacked deeper linguistic analysis or cultural contextualisation, raising concerns about the risk of oversimplifying the rich phonological, morphological, and sociolinguistic structures inherent in SASL. Also, although important, this type of technology is focused on Deaf-to-hearing and not hearing-to-Deaf advancements. Only one of the reviewed studies extended its scope beyond translation and recognition tasks to explore the use of AI for promoting multilingualism within Deaf communities. This study hinted at the broader societal applications and transformative potentials of AI beyond technical translation alone. Socially responsive applications of AI in SASL research remain underexplored.

Another salient finding from the scoping review is the near absence of comprehensive ethical engagement in the existing literature. Few studies documented considerations related to informed consent, bias mitigation, representativity of training data, or active involvement of the Deaf community in the development and validation of AI models. Similarly, discussions around the governance, ownership, and protection of SASL data collected for ML purposes were largely absent. Moreover, the review identified a critical shortage of standardised protocols for video collection, annotation, and data representation in SASL AI studies. The absence of established norms for how SASL signs are recorded, annotated, and transformed into machine-readable data introduces significant variability and potential biases across different studies. Without unified annotation standards, the ability to create interoperable and generalisable ML models for SASL remains constrained. Although speculative, most studies appeared to have been conducted in isolation, without evidence of sustained interdisciplinary collaboration between linguists, computer scientists, Deaf Studies scholars, and members of the Deaf community. This is mentioned as there was no explicit mention of the Deaf involvement in the study process, only as subjects within the research.

A primary theme that emerged is the technological concentration on AI machine translation and recognition systems. Most studies reviewed prioritised the development of computational tools aimed at translating SASL signs into spoken or written language, or at recognising signs through computer vision and neural network technologies. These efforts often centred around model accuracy, algorithmic performance, and technical feasibility, demonstrating a clear engineering-driven orientation in the research. While such technological pursuits are significant, they often operate in relative isolation from deeper linguistic inquiry, with minimal integration of sign language phonology, morphology, syntax, or sociolinguistic variation. The core objective across most studies was functional translation or recognition, rather than linguistic preservation, cultural fidelity, or community empowerment.

Another prominent theme identified is the general absence of attention to the linguistic complexity and sociolinguistic diversity inherent in SASL. Few studies engaged substantively with the rich grammatical structures, spatial grammars, non-manual signals, or dialectal variations that are critical to the authenticity of sign language communication. Dialectical differences influenced by geography, educational background, and community affiliations were largely unrepresented in model development and evaluation. The scarcity of work recognising sociolinguistic variables highlights a gap that risks producing oversimplified, standardised outputs that do not adequately reflect the lived realities of SASL users. This thematic oversight points to an urgent need for interdisciplinary collaboration between linguists and technologists to enhance the depth and accuracy of MLapplications in SASL.

2.5 Limited Ethical Engagement

A critical theme that emerged from the scoping review relates to the limited engagement with ethical considerations. Despite the implications of AI and other ML applications for Deaf communities, few studies incorporated detailed discussions on data ethics, informed consent, bias mitigation, or community consultation. The rights of data subjects, issues of data ownership, and the governance of AI and ML outputs were seldom explicitly addressed. There was little evidence of structured efforts to involve Deaf participants meaningfully in the research process, whether at the stages of data collection, model validation, or application deployment. This gap is particularly concerning given the potential for AI-driven systems to misrepresent, exclude, or harm marginalised groups if ethical safeguards are not proactively embedded.

Most studies appeared to rely on limited or ad hoc datasets, often collected without reference to standardised protocols for video recording, glossing, phonological annotation, or metadata documentation. There was a notable absence of large, representative corpora that would allow for robust, generalisable AI models. Where datasets were mentioned, their collection practices were often not disclosed in sufficient detail to evaluate ethical compliance, cultural representativity, or linguistic robustness. This scarcity of structured data poses a significant bottleneck to technological progress and exacerbates risks of bias, inaccuracy, and exclusion in resulting AI models. There was limited evidence of cumulative knowledge-building, cross-institutional collaboration, or the establishment of shared research agendas. This fragmentation not only slows the pace of innovation but also risks repeating mistakes, overlooking best practices, and failing to integrate critical interdisciplinary insights necessary for responsible AI development.

2.6 Emerging Awareness of the Need for Inclusivity

Despite the limitations observed, an emerging theme is the nascent recognition of the need for greater inclusivity and community engagement. While still underdeveloped, some studies acknowledged the importance of involving Deaf participants in data collection processes or validating the usability of translation systems with Deaf users. There were early signs that researchers are beginning to consider how ML tools should be designed not merely for, but with, Deaf communities. Although such considerations were rare and inconsistently applied, their presence suggests a growing consciousness that future research must move toward participatory and rights-based frameworks.

The literature reveals a limited focus on the long-term sustainability and maintenance of AI and ML tools once developed. Most projects are centred on proof-of-concept or prototype systems, with little discussion of how such technologies would be updated, maintained, or integrated into accessible public platforms over time. The absence of sustainability planning raises concerns about whether the few technological gains made can have a lasting and equitable impact for SASL users, or whether they risk becoming isolated experiments without meaningful application.

A critical opportunity lies in the creation of large-scale, ethically governed, and linguistically diverse SASL datasets. Future research should prioritise the development of corpora that accurately reflect the rich variation within the Deaf community, encompassing dialectal diversity, generational differences, educational backgrounds, and regional signing practices. Such datasets should be constructed through participatory methodologies that centre Deaf individuals as co-researchers and data custodians, not merely as subjects. Establishing transparent protocols for informed consent, data ownership, and usage rights will be essential to ensure that these datasets support both technological development and community empowerment. Rather than treating SASL signs as discrete visual tokens, researchers can develop models that incorporate grammatical structures, spatial syntax, classifier constructions, and non-manual features. This linguistically enriched approach would produce AI systems that better capture the true complexity and nuance of SASL communication, thereby enhancing both model performance and cultural fidelity.

There is an urgent need for the development of standardised protocols for video data collection, annotation, and formatting that are tailored to the specific characteristics of SASL. Future work should focus on creating annotation frameworks grounded in phonological, morphological, and sociolinguistic principles, enabling consistent and meaningful representation of sign language data for computational purposes. Collaborations between linguists, Deaf researchers, and technologists will be crucial in setting these standards, which, in turn, would facilitate data interoperability, cross-study comparisons, and the scaling of AI-related initiatives. The field of Data Science would benefit significantly from the establishment of interdisciplinary research networks that can enable sustained collaboration among linguists, computer scientists, Deaf Studies scholars, ethicists, and members of the Deaf community. Future initiatives should prioritise building long-term partnerships that enable the co-production of knowledge and technology, integrating diverse expertise from the inception of research projects through to their application. Institutional support for interdisciplinary training programmes, joint funding schemes, and cross-disciplinary research centres could help nurture a new generation of scholars capable of navigating the complexities of AI-driven sign linguistics.

2.7 Critical Engagement with Ethical Frameworks

There is a clear opportunity for future research to lead in the development of ethical frameworks specific to the use of AI in Deaf contexts. Scholars and practitioners should work collaboratively with Deaf communities to articulate norms and guidelines for ethical data collection, model deployment, and technology dissemination. Topics such as data sovereignty, algorithmic transparency, bias mitigation, and the rights of signers in digital environments should form core areas of inquiry. Proactively addressing these ethical dimensions would not only protect community interests but also enhance the credibility and societal value of technological innovations. Future work should explore participatory and community-led research models that elevate Deaf individuals from research subjects to co-creators of knowledge. This could involve methodologies such as community-based participatory research (CBPR), Deaf-led design thinking workshops, or collaborative ethnographies that inform AI development. Embedding participatory practices would ensure that technologies respond directly to community needs, aspirations, and concerns, thereby promoting more equitable and impactful outcomes. Beyond translation and recognition tasks, there are vast opportunities for future research to explore how ML can support broader sociolinguistic and cultural objectives. AI could be used to document endangered dialects, model language change over time, support heritage preservation initiatives, and facilitate cross-linguistic analysis among SASLs and regional variants. Such applications would broaden the scope of technological engagement, reinforcing the role of AI not just as a tool for accessibility, but as an instrument for cultural continuity and linguistic research.

An important future direction involves the design of AI systems that are not only functional at the prototype stage but also sustainable, scalable, and openly accessible to the broader Deaf community. Research should focus on developing lightweight, user-friendly applications that can be maintained, updated, and distributed widely across South African contexts, including under-resourced and rural areas. Open-source models, transparent algorithms, and accessible user interfaces would democratise access to AI technologies, ensuring that technological benefits are equitably shared.

Future research must therefore critically investigate the socio-political impacts of AI technologies on the Deaf community. This includes analysing how AI systems may influence language standardisation, educational policies, employment opportunities, and social inclusion. Longitudinal studies that assess the lived experiences of Deaf individuals interacting with AI applications will be crucial for understanding the broader societal consequences of technological interventions and for informing policy development that safeguards linguistic and cultural rights.

2.8 Conclusion

The scoping review conducted in this chapter reveals a field that is simultaneously emergent, fragmented, and charged with significant ethical, linguistic, and technological complexities. The intersection of SASL and AI technologies offers undeniable potential for innovation, accessibility, and cultural preservation. However, the academic landscape, as mapped through this review, reflects a nascent and unevenly developed body of scholarship that is characterised by thematic concentration, ethical gaps, limited linguistic integration, and fragmented research efforts. These findings call for a fundamental rethinking of the ways in which AI is applied to linguistically and culturally rich domains such as SASL. The overwhelming focus of existing studies on translation and recognition systems highlights the dominance of computational objectives over holistic linguistic or community-centred aims. While the development of tools capable of recognising or translating signs is a valuable contribution to technological accessibility, the narrow concentration on technical tasks, often devoid of deeper linguistic and sociolinguistic engagement, risks reducing SASL to a set of visual patterns rather than recognising it as a full-fledged natural language with its own grammatical rules, cultural meanings, and historical depth. The lack of attention to linguistic complexity, including the crucial role of non-manual features, spatial grammar, and classifier constructions, underscores the limitations of current ML applications and points to the urgent need for integrating linguistic theory into AI system design. Equally concerning is the minimal engagement with ethical considerations documented in the literature. The sparse treatment of issues such as informed consent, data ownership, cultural sensitivity, and algorithmic bias reveals a troubling oversight, particularly given the socio-historical marginalisation of Deaf communities.

The risk of exacerbating inequalities through AI tools developed without robust ethical frameworks is not hypothetical; it is an immediate and tangible danger. The absence of structured Deaf community participation in the research process, coupled with a lack of clarity regarding the governance and rights associated with SASL data, compounds the potential harms and reinforces systemic barriers to inclusion. Future research must embed ethics not as an ancillary concern but as a foundational principle guiding all stages of technological development. The challenges identified in the literature further expose significant operational and infrastructural gaps. The scarcity of high-quality, machine-readable, and ethically collected SASL datasets poses a major obstacle to technological progress.

Without representative and culturally grounded data, ML models are likely to remain biased, inaccurate, and unfit for deployment in real-world contexts. Moreover, the lack of standardised protocols for data collection, annotation, and glossing introduces inconsistencies that hinder interoperability and scalability across studies. Addressing these infrastructural gaps demands coordinated efforts among linguists, technologists, Deaf Studies scholars, and Deaf communities themselves, with a view toward creating sustainable, standardised resources that can serve as the backbone of future research and application development. The analysis also highlights the pressing need for interdisciplinary collaboration that moves beyond nominal acknowledgements to the genuine integration of expertise. Sustainable partnerships between linguistic researchers, AI developers, ethical theorists, and Deaf community leaders are essential for developing technologies that are not only technically sophisticated, but also socially responsive and culturally affirming. Such collaborations should be grounded in reciprocal knowledge exchange, mutual respect, and long-term commitment rather than short-term, project-based alliances. The cultivation of interdisciplinary research cultures will play a crucial role in empowering a new generation of researchers equipped to navigate the ethical, linguistic, and technological demands of this complex field. Despite the many challenges, the findings of this review point to substantial opportunities for future growth and innovation. The recognition of SASL as an official language, coupled with the increasing societal awareness of the rights and contributions of Deaf communities, provides a unique historical moment to reshape the trajectory of research at this intersection.

By focusing on the development of representative datasets, the incorporation of linguistic theory into AI and ML model architecture, the standardisation of annotation practices, and the embedding of ethical, participatory methodologies, the field can evolve in ways that not only enhance technological functionality but also uphold linguistic diversity, cultural dignity, and community empowerment. Ultimately, the future of SASL, AI, and ML research hinges on a fundamental reorientation toward inclusivity, interdisciplinarity, and ethical responsibility. Technologies developed without attention to the voices, experiences, and aspirations of the Deaf community risk perpetuating new forms of marginalisation under the guise of innovation. Conversely, technologies co-created with the Deaf community, informed by linguistic expertise, and governed by transparent ethical frameworks have the potential to transform access to information, education, and cultural expression in profound ways. The challenge is not merely to advance technological capabilities, but to do so in a manner that honours the linguistic richness of SASL, protects the rights of its users, and contributes to a more equitable and inclusive technological future.

We therefore outline that the intersection of AI and SASL research is at a crossroads. The decisions made in the coming years - regarding research priorities, methodological approaches, ethical safeguards, and community engagement strategies - will fundamentally shape the contours of Deaf inclusion in the digital age. To ensure that technological innovation serves as a tool for empowerment rather than exclusion, researchers, practitioners, and communities must work together with intentionality, humility, and an unwavering commitment to social justice. By building on the insights and opportunities identified through this scoping review, it is possible to create a new paradigm of AI development that is linguistically informed, ethically grounded, and truly representative of the diverse and vibrant realities of the Deaf community in South Africa.

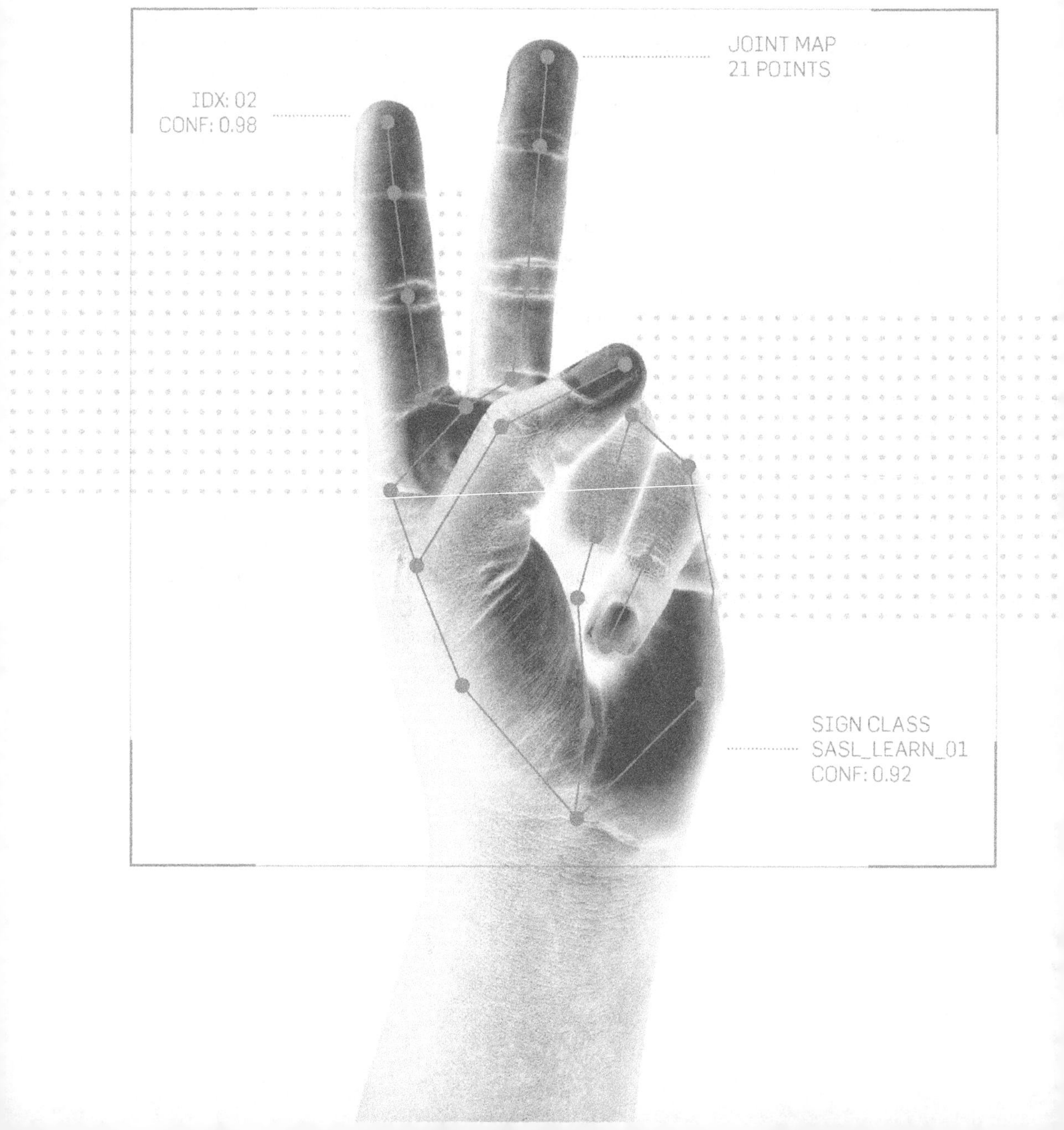
JOINT MAP
21 POINTS
IDX: 02
CONF: 0.98
SIGN CLASS
SASL_LEARN_01
CONF: 0.92

CHAPTER 3

Understanding Sign Language Production

Dr. Herkulaas Combrink

3.1 Introduction

The purpose of this chapter is to explain sign language production for South African Sign Language (SASL). The contents of this technical chapter are based on a framework developed by Moryossef *et al.,* (2023) and Moryossef *et al.,* (2024) for sign language production, an overarching signed language human language technology process. The framework by Moryossef *et al.,* (2023) and Moryossef *et al.,* (2024) explains two processes. This first process is sign language production, which encapsulates converting spoken language into signed pose language. The second process is sign language translation, which is the task of taking some type of signed language input (be it from a video camera or video file) and converting it to spoken language audio. What distinguishes these two processes is the end user.

In the first instance (sign language production), the end user understands a signed language. In the second instance (sign language translation), the end user understands the spoken language. However much of communication is bidirectional, it must be noted that the sign language production process must cater to the Deaf first, before it caters to a hearing person. To put this practically, the applications of such a human language technology, once successful, can guide Deaf workers to receive instructions, can be added to websites to make website interpretation more accessible, and, more fundamentally, provides access to information for a Deaf user. This chapter will only focus on sign language production.

To date, most human language technologies for the Deaf are hearing-centred; that is, that the focus of these technologies is on an output that benefits a hearing community, not a Deaf community or person. Therefore, this chapter will only focus on sign language production and not sign language translation as the Deaf-centred narrative is contextually missing from most human language technology literature. Performing sign language production requires several optimised processes, each with its own distinct challenges and science, with the first step being the conversion of spoken language audio into spoken language text.

3.2 Sign Language Production: Spoken Language Audio into Spoken Language Text

The process of sign language production begins with a person speaking a phrase aloud that gets recorded on a digital device (Rastgoo *et al.,* 2021). Let us assume that the words the person is saying are:

"I'm going to the shop to buy milk".

This spoken sentence is captured via a microphone or audio file input and saved on some type of device, such as a cell phone or a web browser that requires an internet connection. The audio acts as the raw data, containing not just the words but the rhythm, pauses, and intonation of the speaker. Recording a part of audio is dependent on both hardware and software (Bartlett & Bartlett, 2016). The quality of any input has a direct impact on everything that follows in the process (Mukhopadhyay *et al.,* 1997). Once an audio file is recorded, the spoken language audio task commences. The purpose of the spoken language audio task is to collect human speech, which inherently contains a complex array of acoustic features such as tone, pitch, intonation, pace, and volume. If the audio is unclear, distorted, or contains background noise, the transcription in the next stage may be inaccurate, leading to cascading errors throughout the translation. For instance, if a user says:

"I'm going to the shop to buy milk",

in a noisy environment and the system mishears it as:

"I'm going to stop the buying of silk",

the intended meaning diverges significantly. Typically, there are ways to improve the quality of the input file, such as noise filtering, silence trimming, and voice activity detection to isolate the speech components (Khoa, 2012). Ideally, we want accessible human language technologies that can be run on a mobile phone, desktop computer, or tablet, and not an additional piece of hardware for such a task. If such a technology is developed, it needs to be developed with scale in mind, as well as access and accessibility. Due to this reason, the hardware in terms of the microphones for speech detection will differ between devices, and we can and should expect that there will be differences in the quality of sign language production based on the premise of the quality of the original devices.

Once the audio is received, it is processed by an Automatic Speech Recognition (ASR) system to produce a written version of what was said (Yu & Deng, 2016). In this case, the ASR system transcribes the audio into the sentence:

"I'm going to the shop to buy milk".

This written form is easier to work with in computational linguistics and serves as a bridge between spoken and signed modalities. ASR systems are integrated into multiple platforms, in multiple different spoken languages, and advances in natural language processing have made ASR systems very accurate. Unfortunately, ASR systems are not perfect yet, as different accents, speeds of communication, tonality, volume, and other syntactic differences will influence the output of the ASR. The precision of this step is vital; even small transcription errors can significantly distort meaning. Mishearing "shop" as "stop", for example, could lead to a completely different signed translation.

ASR systems rely on acoustic models, language models, and pronunciation dictionaries to map phonemes to words, and must also contend with variations in speaker accents, background noise, speech speed, and intonation. For an ASR system to function optimally, the lexical data from which the models are developed needs to be context and accent specific. That is, if a unique country has a unique set of native accents that are not represented in an ASR, then people communicating into an ASR system will not produce the best text from that communication. Once this is done, language identification as a task needs to take place. For signed language production, this is where the communication starts becoming more complicated.

3.3 Language Identification and Text Normalisation

After obtaining the transcribed sentence from audio, the system identifies the language it is written in, which, in the case of the sentence:

"I'm going to the shop to buy milk",

is English. This is essential because sign languages are not universal. For example, American Sign Language (ASL), British Sign Language (BSL), and SASL are different (Jachova *et al.*, 2008). Correct identification of the signed language ensures that the rest of the pipeline chooses the correct grammatical and cultural structure for the corresponding sign language. This can become rather complex because there are different modalities within a single language. This process signifies the language identification task. The language identification task uses the transcribed text before any semantic or structural processing begins. Misidentifying the language at this stage could result in the entire translation being routed to the wrong target system, producing incorrect or incomprehensible signs. Language identification typically uses statistical models, machine learning classifiers, or transformer-based language models trained on multilingual corpora to analyse n-grams, word frequencies, syntax patterns, or character sequences. As with the development of any language technology, research is needed in these specific areas to improve the contextual relevance for SASL. Another challenge in this area of the sign language production process is the level of code-switched content, that is, where a speaker mixes languages, as we see across different cultures.

Code-switched models need to adapt to the users, and not the users to the models, as this removes user autonomy. In real-time systems, early and accurate identification ensures that the correct linguistic and cultural framework is used for translation, while offline systems may employ more complex ensemble models to achieve higher confidence. Some implementations may skip this step in monolingual applications, but for any scalable, inclusive system supporting diverse user populations, language identification is a foundational gatekeeper. Deaf-centred human language technologies need to be robust, especially since the human language technologies for Deaf people have not been as well-resourced as hearing-based systems, such as large language models and transformers within ASR systems, as in social media. Once the language, with its nuance and context, has been correctly identified, the language normalisation text tasks begins. Text normalisation means simplifying and standardising the sentence by removing filler words or contractions is the primary goal. Practically put, the sentence:

"I'm going to the shop to buy milk",

would be expanded to:

"I am going to the shop to buy milk",

and cleaned to remove any disfluencies. Normalisation ensures consistency in how sentences are interpreted and reduces ambiguity for later stages. Spoken language, when transcribed verbatim, often contains numerous irregularities, including filler words ("um", "like", "you know"), disfluencies, contractions, colloquialisms, incomplete phrases, and inconsistent punctuation. For instance, an ASR system might transcribe a sentence like:

"I'm uh I'm gonna go gonna go to the shop, right, ok, right?",

which, without normalisation, is difficult to translate directly into a clear and grammatically coherent signed language equivalent. For example, without the normalisation step, "I'm" might be finger-spelled as "I" and "M";the slang equivalent of "uh" might not be in the model; and then "gonna" and "go" and "gonna" and "go" repeated would appear incoherent, as the "gonna" would most probably be finger-spelled, while the "go" could contextually mean to leave, or come towards something. The double "right" would not be interpreted as a validation but rather as "correct" resulting in a very incoherent sentence in the final sign language production, even though it reflects what the person said. Therefore, the normalisation systematically processes such input to yield a clean, structured, and semantically accurate version of what was said (Leaman *et al.,* 2015). Normalisation not only removes extraneous or redundant elements but also expands contractions ("I'm" to "I am"), standardises verb forms, resolves slang ("gonna" to "going to"), and ensures consistency in case, punctuation, and formatting. Importantly, normalised text reduces ambiguity and variability in expression, which is essential for deterministic or rule-based systems, as well as for training data in ML models (Weiss & Indurkhya, 1995). A caveat in this normalisation is the bias that is introduced within this process (Heijungs *et al.*, 2007). The context and meaning of the system would be based on the way the models are trained and the type of meaning the sentence wants to evaluate for (Hassan & Mahmood, 2018; Hodosh *et al.*, 2013).

A further complication of text normalisation is the multilingual nature of the spoken language in question (Bigi, 2011). Normalisation must also account for language-specific grammar and morphology (Zhang *et al.*, 2019). In the context of sign language translation, normalisation is even more vital because sign languages do not follow spoken language syntax and often omit certain function words entirely. Therefore, the goal of this task is not to enforce rigid grammatical correctness according to spoken language standards, but rather to produce a version of the input that is semantically complete, unambiguous, and well-suited for subsequent translation into glosses and SignWriting.

Advanced normalisation systems may use natural language processing techniques such as named entity recognition, dependency parsing, and language modelling to better understand context, especially in longer passages (Alonso *et al.*, 2021). ML also plays an important part in this process, as multiple context-specific models need to be developed. Furthermore, normalisation can serve as a point of intervention for accessibility-aware design by adjusting phrasing for clarity, detecting and flagging emotionally charged or culturally sensitive content, and simplifying complex syntactic constructions for better representation in the target signed language. For instance, at this stage of the process, sentiment analysis, topic modelling, and misinformation detection can take place so that they may be further studied. In real-time systems, this step must be performed quickly and with high confidence, often using lightweight rule-based or hybrid models, while in offline or batch systems, more computationally intensive deep learning models may be employed for context-aware normalisation. Once the text is normalised, the sentence splitting and glossing can take place.

3.4 Sentence Splitter, Glossing, and SignWriting

The sentence splitter task functions as a key structural component in the spoken-to-signed language translation pipeline, responsible for dividing normalised text into discrete, syntactically and semantically coherent segments. In other words, the original sentence is then split into smaller sections for further processing. Typically, sentences or clauses can be independently and accurately processed in subsequent stages. While spoken language often flows in an unbroken stream of words, it contains natural boundaries that indicate shifts in meaning, topic, or grammatical structure. These boundaries are easy to identify in words, such as those you are reading now, as there is a definitive start and stop with each word. These boundaries, however, are not always marked by explicit punctuation in raw or even normalised transcriptions, especially in spontaneous speech. The room for error in real-time systems also increases significantly if the normalisation is not perfect. For instance, consider the following normalised sentence:

"I am going to the shop to buy milk, and I will also fix the car after I go to your place".

Though grammatically correct, it contains multiple ideas with distinct actions and timeframes that, in igned language, would often be separated for clarity, facial grammar, and appropriate non-manual signalling. The sentence splitter would therefore analyse this sentence and divide the sentence into its separate clauses, converting it to:

"I am going to the shop to buy milk",

"I will also fix the car",

"after I go to your place".

Each of these units can then be translated more effectively into glosses or sign animation sequences. A further complication would be to split hand movements that transition from sign. In other words, when a sign is made, there is a transition period from one sign to the next. In human language technology, the transition is not important; the word or phrase is. So, when people sign, the correct start and stop time of a sign to be recorded. This is a difficult task. Without this segmentation, the system might attempt to translate the entire sentence as one unit, resulting in an unnatural or unintelligible signed output. For spoken languages, this does not pose a major problem as one can divide these sentences using punctuation and spaces between words, but in a signed language, this is a major problem if not addressed properly. Sentence splitting can be performed using rule-based methods that rely on punctuation and conjunctions; however, more generalisable implementations use natural language processing techniques, such as part-of-speech tagging, syntactic parsing, or transformer-based models, to infer boundaries in ambiguous cases, for example when a speaker omits punctuation or speaks in run-on sentences.

In multilingual contexts, sentence splitting must also be language-aware, adapting to the grammatical conventions of the source language. Furthermore, in real-time systems, sentence splitting must operate incrementally, detecting clause breaks on the fly based on pauses in speech, discourse markers, or predictive models, whereas, in offline systems, a full-text view allows for more accurate segmentation using contextual information. From a sign language translation perspective, accurate sentence splitting is essential not only for linguistic precision but also for visual timing, as sign languages rely heavily on facial expressions, body posture, and spatial referencing to distinguish between clauses and ideas. Improper segmentation can lead to confusing animations where non-manual signals run together, making it difficult for viewers to understand whether a signer is indicating sequential actions, conditional statements, or different subjects. Although not discussed here, it must be noted that segmentation requires multiple processes running in parallel to determine the best segmentation, based on the system and architecture of the segmentation process being implemented. In some implementations, sentence splitting may also tag sentence types, such as declarative, interrogative, or imperative, which inform facial grammar in the signing output. Sentence splitting informs the glossing stage of the process, which is vital for sign language production. Glossing is the process that distils the sentence into core meaning words that align with how sign language expresses ideas. So:

"I am going to the shop to buy milk",

might become:

"I SHOP MILK",

in gloss. Itis not word-for-word but concept-for-concept, stripping grammar that sign language expresses differently, such as tense or aspect, and reorganising the sentence into a structure native to sign languages. A fundamental misnomer and assumption among hearing people is that a sign language follows the same structure of communication as a spoken language. It does not. Part of this misconception lies at the core of the human language technology infodemic and may help to explain why technological development, in general, has been so misinformed in this area of research.

The glossing stage is essential for the sign language production process because it adapts spoken language logic into a format that can be used to drive sign generation technologies, whether through animation, avatars, or notation systems. In practice, this transformation can be achieved using rule-based systems built on linguistic studies of sign languages, or through statistical and neural machine translation models trained on parallel corpora of spoken language sentences and their gloss equivalents. More advanced systems may also tag each gloss with grammatical features such as part of speech, tense, subject-object alignment, and classifier type, enabling more nuanced generation of sign movements later in the pipeline. Furthermore, glossing is not always a one-to-one mapping. This means that a single English word like "building", might correspond to multiple signs depending on context - for example, whether it refers to a large building, a house, a warehouse, a garage, a hut, and so on. Contextual disambiguation is crucial. Glossing can therefore fundamentally differ between different regions of the same language, because the context is fundamentally different (Figure 3.1).

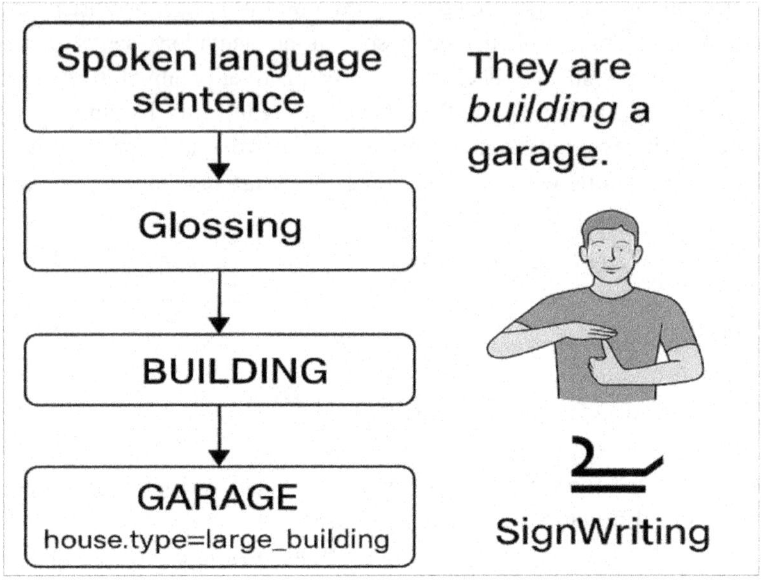

***Figure 3.1**: Example of spoken language to gloss.*

In educational and linguistic settings, glosses are frequently used as a learning aid to teach sign language grammar to hearing individuals or to annotate signing videos for research. In translation systems, however, glosses serve a more dynamic role as an intermediate representation that feeds directly into sign generation, such as pose sequencing, SignWriting rendering, or 3D avatar animation. The modularity of this step also allows it to function as a pivot point in multilingual systems. Once spoken inputs from various languages are normalised and mapped to glosses, the rest of the translation pipeline can operate largely independent of the source language. Ultimately, the glosses enable the abstract, highly contextual structures of natural spoken language to be systematically restructured into a compact, semantically rich format that is optimised for visual-spatial rendering. It acts as a form of linguistic compression, distilling meaning while preserving communicative intent, and ensuring that what gets animated or displayed in sign language is accurate, intelligible, and culturally appropriate. Once the language is glossed, it can be converted into SignWriting.

SignWriting is a visual writing system that represents sign languages in a written format (Sutton, 1990). Once the text is in SignWriting notation, the tasks to follow are a direct implementation of the SignWriting process and no longer work with any of the original audio. In other words, until SignWriting for the audio is developed, the process up to this point works with the audio- to-text tasks (Sutton, 1990). The SignWriting task occupies a unique and linguistically significant position within the spoken-to-signed language translation pipeline, functioning as a formal notation system that transcribes signed languages into a visual script capable of encoding handshape, movement, orientation, facial expression, and spatial structure. Unlike glosses, which are simplifications using words from spoken languages to describe signs, SignWriting is a writing system developed specifically for sign languages, analogous to how alphabets represent spoken language sounds. After the input has been processed into glosses, the SignWriting task takes those conceptual representations, like:

"I SHOP MILK",

and converts them into visual symbols arranged spatially on a two-dimensional plane to reflect how signs are performed in physical space. Each component of a sign, such as the position and orientation of the hands, the shape of the fingers, the path of movement, and accompanying facial expressions, is encoded using a combination of symbols drawn from the SignWriting system's extensive symbolic inventory. This symbolic structure is not linear, as in in spoken languages, but is instead arranged spatially to reflect the geometry and simultaneity of signed communication.

SignWriting enables a level of precision and expressiveness that glosses alone cannot achieve, particularly in capturing non-manual signals like raised eyebrows (used to indicate yes/no questions), mouth movements, or head tilts, features essential for grammatical clarity in most signed languages. For signed languages, the value of this task lies not only in its ability to preserve the linguistic richness of sign languages but also in its potential to serve as a machine-readable intermediate representation between linguistic processing and visual rendering stages. As mentioned earlier, this can also be achieved through glosses; however, glossing fails to capture a lot of the 3D intonation required for contextual expression.

From a computational standpoint, the generation of SignWriting symbols may involve template matching, rule-based mappings, or neural-symbolic models trained on aligned gloss-SignWriting datasets. In practice, however, the availability of such datasets is limited, which has historically slowed the development of fully automated SignWriting generation systems. Tools like SignPuddle and SignMaker offer human-in-the-loop interfaces for producing SignWriting, but automating this process remains a key research challenge. Despite this, SignWriting has already proven valuable in education, particularly among Deaf communities who use it to read and write in their native sign languages, as well as in linguistics for transcription and preservation. In translation pipelines, it offers a distinct pathway alongside avatar-based animation.

Another important possibility for SignWriting is that it supports multilingual representation across various signed languages. SignWriting captures unique grammars and vocabularies, enabling the use of sign language, rather than spoken language, as scaffolding in generating corpora. This is especially important for empowering signers to engage with written content in their own linguistic modality, rather than relying on translations into spoken language text. Overall, the SignWriting task embodies a powerful convergence of linguistic fidelity, visual structure, and accessibility. By encoding the spatial and kinetic aspects of sign language in a structured, symbolic script, it provides both a machine-interpretable and human-readable format that reinforces the authenticity, clarity, and cultural integrity of the signed message being translated and displayed.

3.5 Illustration, Description, and Pose Sequence

The illustration tasks represent an alternative or complementary output pathway in the spoken-to-signed language translation pipeline, tasked with generating static visual representations of signs, typically drawn or digitally rendered images that depict the position, orientation, and movement of the hands, body, and face at key moments within a sign. This task serves a particularly important role in scenarios where animated outputs, such as avatar-driven or pose-based signing, are unavailable, too resource-intensive, or not required. Ideally, with the right technology, outputs should be human, lifelike, and aesthetically pleasing. However, with current technological constraints, these expectations cannot be met. Therefore, by using SignWriting symbols, glosses, or structured pose data as input, the illustration tasks produce one or more frames that capture the visual essence of a sign. For instance, in our continuing example, where the input sentence:

"I am going to the shop to buy milk",

has been converted into the gloss sequence:

"I SHOP MILK",

and then into SignWriting, the illustration task might output a three-panel image, with one panel showing a person pointing to their chest for "I," another illustrating an outward hand movement depicting a directional sign toward a building shape for "SHOP", and a final panel illustrating "MILK".

Unlike the dynamic rendering used in pose animation, illustrations aim to distil each sign into a small number of frames. Conceptually, this is like sentence splitting, except that the illustration is made directly from the SignWriting or other modality, such as glossing. These images are often simplified, showing clear handshapes, directional arrows, and expressive cues, such as raised eyebrows or mouth positions, with minimal background distractions. Their primary utility is educational and communicative, allowing users, especially sign language learners, children, or those with slower internet connections, to grasp the structure of signs without needing video playback. In some systems, the illustration may also serve as a fallback when a given sign is not available in the avatar animation database, or when rendering is delayed due to bandwidth or processing constraints.

Illustrations are important for bridging literacy gaps, especially among Deaf users who may have limited proficiency in written and spoken languages. When paired with SignWriting or glosses, illustrations can help reinforce learning by providing both a symbolic and visual representation of a sign. In printed or offline materials, such as textbooks, posters, or instruction cards, illustrations remain the most practical method for depicting signs. They are also vital for archival or accessibility purposes, particularly in settings where animated avatars are not appropriate (such as official documentation, forms, or signage).

Unfortunately, SignWritting and glossing, for example, are not explicitly taught across all curricula, and the skills to transfer this knowledge are not readily available (Amin *et al.*, 2021; Rathkey, 2019). From a human language technology perspective, simply having large bodies of corpora in glossed or SignWritting is already a major resource that can enhance any signed language (Bianchini, 2021).

From a technical standpoint, challenges in the illustration tasks are all intended to include consistency in visual style, anatomical accuracy, clarity of movement depiction, and cultural appropriateness across different sign languages. However, a major flaw in the design of the visual style is that it was developed to "work", rather than to provide full functional utility. For a person who is only fluent in their respective signed language, the transition to a from a human figure to a comically illustrated figure represents a significant gap. Therefore, illustrations, and technology based on illustrations, do require training to be followed and understood. Signs often involve subtle distinctions in palm orientation, finger extension, or facial expression that must be faithfully represented to avoid misinterpretation. In multilingual deployments, this task must also manage variant signs for the same concept across languages (e.g., the sign for "SHOP" in ASL versus SASL) and select or generate illustrations accordingly. Some systems may allow user feedback or community input to validate illustrations and enrich the database over time. Alternatively, or in addition, the system can produce a textual description of how to perform the signs. For "GO", it might generate:

"Extend right hand, palm down, move forward".

These descriptions are particularly helpful for learners, visually impaired users, and for linguistic annotation. This approach provides clarity on what the sign should look like without needing visual media. There are instances where some people have a visual and auditory impairment, and for this reason, these types of technologies need to be developed. The description task, as opposed to the illustration task, translates glosses, SignWriting symbols, or pose data into natural language descriptions that articulate the components of each sign in a form readable by humans, especially those who may not be fluent in the signed language being presented. In this series of tasks, after a sentence such as:

"I am going to the shop to buy milk",

has been converted to a gloss:

"I SHOP MILK",

the description task would focus on generating detailed instructions, for example:

*"For 'I', use your dominant hand in a pointing gesture, index finger extended,
pointing toward your chest. For 'STORE', hold both hands near your temples
in an 'O' handshape and flick them forward twice…."*

These descriptions allow a reader to mentally visualise and potentially reproduce the signs without relying on images or video. This textual rendering is particularly useful in contexts where visual media are not supported, such as screen readers for blind or visually impaired users, environments with strict bandwidth limitations, or print-based accessibility materials. It also plays a pedagogical role, helping learners of sign language better understand the physical and grammatical components of each sign, as literacy levels among the Deaf tend to be low across multiple contexts. While illustrations or avatars show what a sign looks like, descriptions explain how to produce it, often including subtle linguistic cues such as facial expressions, signing space (e.g., neutral space, near the body, above the head), and hand movement directions (e.g., "arc upward," "twist wrist inward"). For instance, a yes/no question in SASL requires raised eyebrows, which the description task would include as:

"Raise your eyebrows and tilt your head slightly forward while signing."

Technically, describing all the features in a word can be powered by rule-based systems, where each gloss is linked to a pre-written explanatory text stored in a dictionary, or it may dynamically generate descriptions using template-based natural language generation (McRoy *et al.,* 2003). The problem with rule-based systems is the amount of context and rules that need to be produced so that a sufficient system may be developed (Ligeza, 2006). For this to work and function optimally, it requires a lot of skill, time, and training (Nalepa & Bobek, 2014). ML, on the other hand, can also assist with some of these tasks; however, for it to function optimally with description tasks, substantial research, contextual knowledge, and skills development are required (Aslam *et al.,* 2017).

In more sophisticated systems, neural language models trained on aligned gloss-description pairs could be used to create adaptive, context-aware outputs, especially for complex or compound signs (De Coster & Dambre, 2022). Neural language models become essential when dealing with classifiers (signs that describe categories of objects through handshape and motion) or spatial verbs, which often change depending on the referents and locations described earlier in the sentence (Kulmizev & Nivre, 2022). In multilingual systems, description tasks must therefore be localised to the specific context, not just linguistically but also culturally. The way signs are described may vary between languages, not only because of vocabulary differences but also because some cultures may prefer different levels of anatomical detail, formality, or instructional tone (LeMaster & Monaghan, 2004). Furthermore, the same gloss might require multiple descriptions depending on dialect or regional variation. For instance, the sign for "SHOP" in SASL has regional variants that may use different handshapes or motions, and the model must select the appropriate variant based on user settings or context detection.

From an accessibility and inclusion standpoint, the description task holds particular importance (Tuveri, 2024). The description task enables people with limited or no access to video, due to technical, cognitive, or physical barriers, to still receive information about how signing occurs. The description task is also valuable for integration into multi-modal systems, such as those combining sign translation with subtitles or screen readers, as well as for creating training materials, linguistic research data, and automated testing frameworks. Due to the nature of descriptions as text, descriptions are easily logged, indexed, and versioned. They also facilitate traceability in system development and can support transparency in AI-based sign generation, allowing users to see how a given sign is derived.

The core of animation begins with a pose sequence (Tan *et al.,* 2024). Using the gloss or SignWriting, the system generates a sequence of body poses for each sign. For:

"I SHOP MILK",

this would involve defining where the signer's arms, hands, and body are positioned over time. These poses are represented as joint coordinates, like those found in motion capture systems, providing the skeleton for animation. The Pose Sequence tasks represent the transitions previously conveyed through glosses, SignWriting, or descriptions, into a structured, time-based series of body positions that simulate the actual performance of sign language. These sequences are composed of articulated pose frames, each specifying the spatial coordinates and orientations of key body joints over time, including the shoulders, elbows, wrists, fingers, head, torso, and facial landmarks. Pose sequencing marks the transition from abstract linguistic representation to embodied, visual expression (Prabhudesai *et al.,* 2020). For instance, following the gloss sequence:

"I SHOP MILK",

the pose sequence task generates a temporal series of skeleton-like poses where frame-by-frame the avatar or animation system knows where the right hand points to the chest for "I", how both hands perform the movement for "SHOP", and then transition to the signs for "MILK". Each of these is broken into incremental postures that, when animated in sequence, visually communicate the intended message in natural sign language.

At its core, the pose sequence builds a 3D representation of motion over time. Motion is important, and therefore the time (temporal component) is important (Brown, 1995). For both motion and the temporal component of signs, time series analysis and other temporal analyses can justify the outputs of these models (Huang *et al.,* 2022). Another aspect of pose sequencing is the representation into multiple formats, such as 2D joint coordinates, 3D mesh rigging, or more abstract kinematic representations, depending on the animation (Humphrey *et al.,* 2022). The source of these sequences can be derived through a variety of methods. In rule-based systems, glosses are mapped to pre-recorded or synthetically generated movement templates (Goyal & Goyal, 2016). In more advanced systems, this process can be powered by neural motion generation models trained on aligned gloss-pose corpora, in which a sequence of glosses is used to condition a motion synthesis model that outputs a smooth, continuous pose stream (Yu *et al.,* 2025; Agrawal *et al.,* 2024). The challenge in this process lies in capturing the grammatical and expressive richness of sign languages, which encode not just meaning but also emotional tone, discourse structure, and syntactic elements such as role-shifting or conditional clauses through body movement and facial expression (Prokott *et al.,* 2021). It should be noted that, at this point, both the motion and temporal aspects of signs contain some form of inference based on the SignWriting or glosses, which may lead to bias in the outputs (Figure 3.2).

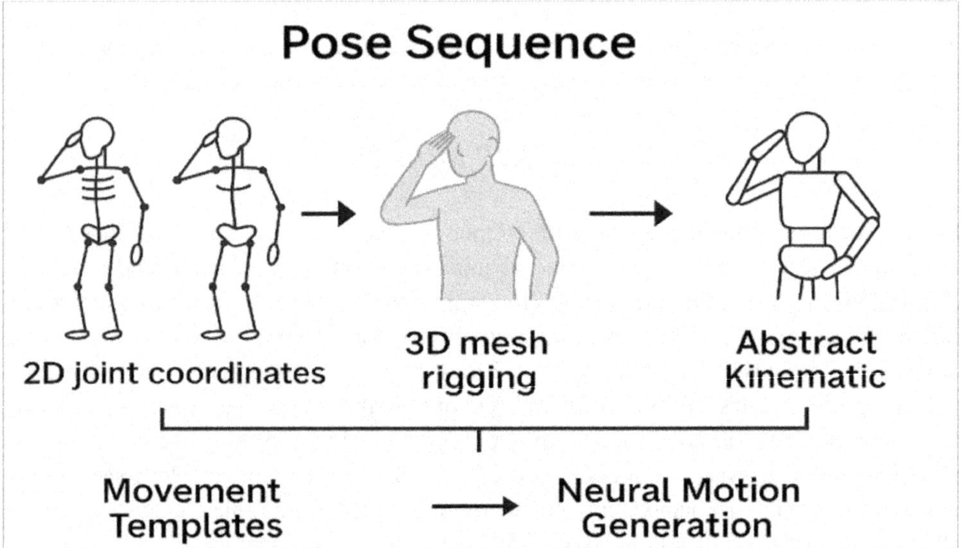

Figure 3.2*: From pose data to animation.*

The pose sequence must, therefore, balance timing and synchronisation of the signs by deciding how long each sign should last, when transitions should begin, and how overlapping gestures (e.g., simultaneous hand movements or facial expressions) are coordinated (Liu *et al.,* 2024). The pose sequence will differ between models and individuals and should fundamentally be adjustable to cater to the users' needs. Another key consideration in this task is spatial referencing and role shifting, which are both essential elements of sign language grammar that use the signing space to refer to subjects, objects, or narrative perspectives (Emmorey *et al.,* 2001). Systems that fail to account for this risk may produce signs that are technically accurate in shape but incorrect in meaning due to spatial ambiguity (Leveson, 2015).

To make the signing more lifelike, the skeletal pose data is passed through a model that adds visual details such as body shape, clothing, skin, and lighting. So instead of seeing a wireframe, users might see a 3D human figure wearing a shirt and jeans, performing the "GO" motion. To generate such an image, a realistic human-like figure may be created using a rich appearance attribute such as skin tone, clothing, facial features, lighting, and stylistic texture (Jia *et al.,* 2022).

While pose sequences encode how a sign is performed, describing the timing, direction, and spatial positioning of body parts, they do so in a minimal, skeletal form. A pose appearance takes this structural blueprint and wraps it in a layer of visual realism to produce a lifelike rendering that can be recognised, interpreted, and related to by human viewers. For example, the skeletal movement generated for the gloss sequence:

"I GO SHOP MILK",

becomes a dynamic visualisation of a person, perhaps wearing casual clothing, with human-like hands and facial expressions, performing each sign naturally and believably.

From here on, all the tasks associated with the sign language production process focus on optimising visualisations (Elliot *et al.,* 2008). Optimising visualisations related to sign language production includes elements that smooth transitions to make signs more fluent, models that improve 3D rendering to make the models more lifelike, and functions that assist the overall user experience. Each of these processes is specific to the context in which the human language technology is developed, and not merely about getting the technology to work. Visual representation, the specific signed language in question, the available technologies in the region, and most importantly, the needs of the Deaf communities will ultimately drive these processes. Therefore, no universal blueprint can be designed, from a human language technology perspective, for what each of these language systems would look like. Importantlythere is currently a difference between Human Language Technologies developed with the end user as a hearing person, and those developed for a person from a Deaf culture (Figure 3.3).

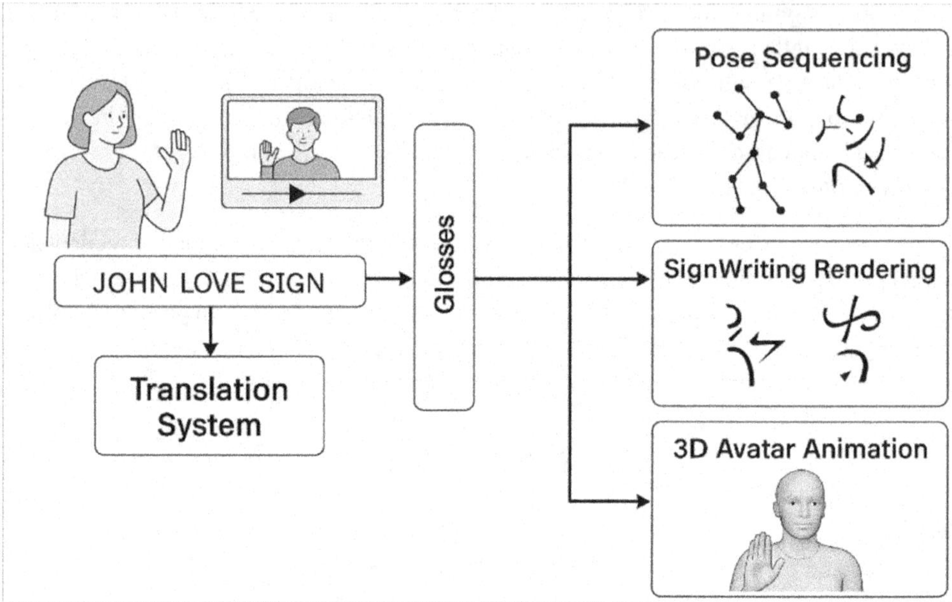

***Figure 3.3**: Glosses enable visual sign production.*

Given the framework set out by Moryossef *et al.,* (2023) and Moryossef *et al.,* (2024) for sign language production, each specific sign language needs to develop its own sign language production pipeline. What is not discussed in this book is the process of sign language translation, as this has been extensively researched (Liang *et al.,* 2023). To understand the Deaf infodemic and move towards addressing it, we must begin with information based on what is and is not scientifically discussed or focused on in this domain. In the context of SASL, there are major challenges in both processes, not just in sign language production. These challenges will be outlined in the next chapter.

CHAPTER 4

Challenges in SASL Production

Dr. Herkulaas Combrink and Ms Gloria Motshoeneng

4.1 Introduction

The purpose of this chapter is to critically examine the current research gaps and challenges in the development of South African Sign Language (SASL) production and related human language technologies. As technological advancements open new possibilities for multimodal human language processing, SASL remains significantly under-represented within existing computational frameworks, particularly with respect to SASL production tasks. This chapter systematically explores the major obstacles encountered at each stage of the SASL production pipeline, from converting normalised text into glosses and splitting sentences for SignWriting, to generating fluent pose sequences, producing accurate sign illustrations, and synthesising human-like signers through various forms of illustration.

Special emphasis is placed on the complex relationship between demographic diversity, training data limitations, and context-specific requirements, which together influence the quality, accessibility, and appropriateness of generated outputs. These gaps are rooted in current literature and build upon the sign language production frameworks set out by Moryossef *et al.,* (2023) and Moryossef *et al.,* (2024).

4.2 Challenges in Normalised Text to Gloss Conversion for SASL

One of the foundational steps in developing advanced machine translation and human language technologies for SASL involves the conversion of normalised written text into gloss representations. For SASL, there are no repositories of glossed SASL data large enough to build a model that can perform this task automatically. The structure of SASL differs from that of written or spoken English, upon which most available text corpora are based. SASL uses a topic-comment structure, makes extensive us of classifiers, and conveys temporal and conditional relationships through spatial modifications and non-manual signals, such as eyebrow movements and subtle mouth movements.

Normalised text, which smooths out the complexities and ambiguities of natural language for computational purposes, tends to favour linear, spoken language syntax. Spoken language syntax does not contain spatial and temporal elements within the language, and so these are not captured in the text for sign languages. In the case of SASL, there are no glossing metrics to uniformly capture and categorise all this context effectively. While glossing systems exist for several international sign languages, SASL-specific glossing practices remain relatively underdeveloped and inconsistently applied. Different researchers and institutions may use varying conventions for representing handshapes, classifier constructions, directional verbs, or non-manual markers. This inconsistency introduces significant noise and ambiguity into training data, making it even more difficult for automated systems to learn reliable conversion mappings.

The unintended consequence of this also creates fragmented schools of thought within the human language technology space for signed languages. The absence of a widely accepted glossing standard for SASL not only hinders AI but also complicates human annotation, evaluation, and cross-corpus interoperability. Compounding these challenges is the fact that glosses are inherently a poor representation of sign languages, as the gloss is just a fit-for-purpose transition between Sign and spoken languages. Thus, even a perfect text-to-gloss conversion may fail to capture the full richness of SASL discourse.

AI models trained solely on glosses risk developing brittle representations that cannot generalise well to the nuances of real-world signing, where multiple layers of meaning are conveyed simultaneously through hand configuration, movement, facial expression, and body posture. Most available gloss datasets for sign languages are limited, domain-specific, and often focused on European or North American Sign Languages such as American Sign Language (ASL) or British Sign Language (BSL). SASL, with its unique linguistic features, regional variations, and sociocultural specificity, is vastly under-represented in existing computational resources. Without sufficiently large and diverse training datasets, AI models cannot learn the mappings needed to convert normalised text into gloss sequences that are grammatically, semantically, and culturally appropriate for SASL users. Words and their meanings will differ between the languages, and contextual usage may not align with that of other languages, as SASL is a distinct language in its own right. Therefore, semantic mismatch between English and SASL lexical items is possible given that a single English word, for example, may correspond to multiple distinct signs in SASL, or the other way around. These differences, contexts, and modalities may encompass a range of English words or concepts. Simple word-level alignments are insufficient. For scholars working directly with SASL and any other signed language, the signed language is its own communication system. The unique communication system presented by a signed language makes the fundamental method of conveying and receiving meaning different from those of, for example, English. Just simply transferring a word from SASL to another South African language, or the other way around, is not enough for effective translation. In South Africa, a large portion of the country's languages are considered low-resourced languages, and SASL is one of them. Several attempts have started to produce more language resources for under-represented languages in the Southern African context, but as literature suggests, there is still a lot of work needed to justify a true representation of most African languages, spoke or signed languages. As a result, efforts to develop normalised text-to-gloss systems for SASL must contend not only with technical challenges but also with infrastructural gaps in linguistic documentation, corpus development, and computational resource allocation.

Challenges also exist within the scientific domain related to the task of glossing SASL from normalised text. One of these challenges relates to the linguistic mismatch that is observed. The context of one language is not effectively captured in another (Ebling *et al.,* 2015). Tied to this, is the ambiguity and semantic mismatch that may occur because the glosses will look identical when glossed from different languages. Given the nature of SASL, these classifications have subtle gestures that are simply lost in a glossed version of any text (Starner, 1995).

Without sufficient data, models cannot learn the complex linguistic mappings needed for reliable gloss generation. Semantic ambiguity adds another layer of complexity. Single words in any South African language may correspond to multiple SASL signs depending on context, and single SASL signs may encompass multiple English concepts (Starner, 1995). This one-to-many or many-to-one relationship creates high levels of uncertainty in automatic mapping processes. Glosses all omit facial expressions, head movements, and body posture cues, which are essential for conveying grammatical relations and affective nuances in SASL (Brentari, 2011). The lack of standardised glossing conventions further complicates this task. This does not suggest that SASL needs standardisation, but rather that the methods used for glossing require buy-in so that there can be a consensus among scientists in the domain. Different researchers, educational institutions, and datasets apply glosses differently, making it difficult to ensure consistency across training data and model outputs (Johnston & Schembri, 2007). Evaluation challenges persist because traditional translation metrics are poorly suited for assessing gloss quality (Rathkey, 2019). These challenges illustrate that normalised text to gloss conversion for SASL requires more than traditional machine translation techniques (Table 4.1).

Table 4.1: Challenges in normalised text to glossed SASL

Challenge	Description	Example Reference
Grammatical Structure Mismatch	Signed languages like SASL use spatial, simultaneous grammars unlike linear text structures.	Factors to consider when making lexical comparisons of Sign Languages: Notes from an ongoing comparison of German Sign Language and Swiss German Sign Language (Ebling *et al.,* 2015).
Dataset Scarcity	Very few parallel corpora exist linking normalised text and glosses for sign languages like SASL.	Documentary and corpus approaches to sign language research (Fenlon *et al.,* 2015).
Semantic Ambiguity	Words in text can map to multiple glosses, or multiple signs may correspond to a single word.	Visual recognition of ASL using hidden Markov models (Starner, 1995).

Challenge	Description	Example Reference
Loss of Non-Manual Information	Glosses often omit critical facial expressions, mouth movements, and body grammar cues.	Sign languages (Brentari, D. 2011).
Lack of Glossing Standardisation	No universal glossing system exists, and inconsistencies hamper training and evaluation.	Australian Sign Language: An Introduction (Johnston & Schembri, 2007).
Evaluation Challenges	Current translation metrics (e.g., BLEU) are ill-suited for assessment of gloss correctness.	*ASL-gloss be used as an instructional tool to teach written English to the Deaf (*Rathkey, 2019).

SASL is a community-owned language with deep cultural significance for South African Deaf communities. Data collection, annotation, and model development must be conducted with community consent, participation, and benefit-sharing at every stage. Building large, annotated corpora requires these challenges to be addressed. Until there is a designated framework in place, the normalisation of text-to-glossed SASL will remain a problem. An attempt to create such a framework is proposed by Combrink *et al.,* (2025), in which the handling of SASL data, including issues of data management, ethics, and licencing, becomes vital for the advancement of SASL resources in human language technological applications.

4.3 SignWriting for SASL

Up until this point, the focus has been on text that can represent a hearing-centred perspective on a signed language. However, this glossed-type language is by no means a representation of the written form of a signed language. SignWriting, a visual writing system, offers a powerful and increasingly indispensable tool for representing the rich complexity of signed languages in a durable, accessible written form (Sutton, 1990). Designed to capture the movements, handshapes, orientations, facial expressions, and body positions that comprise the grammar and lexicon of signed languages, SignWriting is a modality-specific approach that contrasts with the gloss-based systems historically used to approximate signed discourse (Sutton, 1990; Sutton & Frost, 2008).

Unlike glosses, which rely on word-for-word or phrase-for-phrase substitutions into spoken or written languages such as English, SignWriting operates entirely within the visual-spatial modality of sign languages themselves, preserving the simultaneity, spatial indexing, and embodied grammar that are central to SASL, among other signed languages. Although not widely accepted, some researchers have argued that SignWriting should be the lexical system for signed languages, just like text is the modality for most spoken languages in Southern Africa. In SASL, as in many other signed languages, information is frequently conveyed simultaneously across multiple articulators and along multiple spatial planes (Pfau *et al.,* 2012).

SignWriting is a graphical convention that allows for the depiction of simultaneous events, such as a hand moving while an eyebrow raises, preserving the layered structure of meaning that is characteristic of natural signed discourse (Sutton & Frost, 2008; Hanke, 2004). In other words, SignWriting in and of itself, is uniquely positioned to serve as the text equivalent for signed languages, rather than merely glossing a language into its signed language equivalent, which loses context (Figure 4.1):

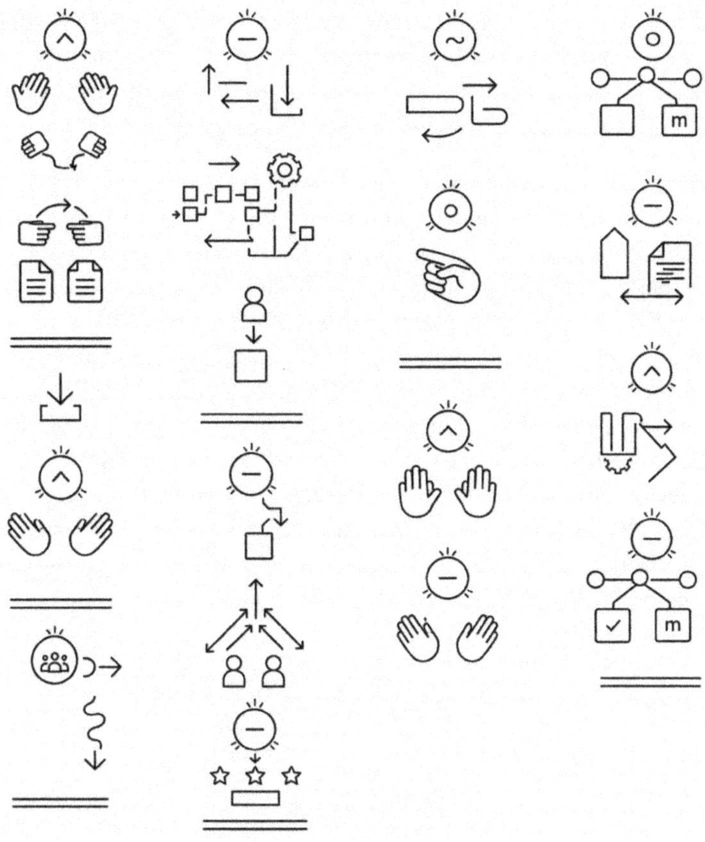

Figure 4.1*: Example of SignWriting context captured.*

Despite these advantages, the adoption of SignWriting in computational linguistics and AI for sign languages, including SASL, remains limited. Much of the current infrastructure in sign language processing continues to rely on gloss-based corpora, due to the relative ease of gloss annotation compared with full SignWriting transcription. However, as efforts intensify to build more authentic and community-centred technologies, the importance of incorporating SignWriting into annotation, modelling, and translation pipelines grows increasingly clear (Efthimiou *et al.,* 2012).

Unfortunately, resource limitations constrain innovation in the domain of SignWriting justification, research, and validity as a linguistic system of SASL. SignWriting in SASL is a complex, underexplored, and urgently necessary area of research. Over the past two decades, research into SignWriting has expanded from small educational initiatives into broader interdisciplinary fields encompassing linguistics, computer science, digital humanities, and accessibility studies (Fenlon *et al.,* 2015).

Contemporary research into SignWriting has focused primarily on SignWriting's role in promoting sign language literacy, SignWriting's application in corpus creation for linguistic analysis, and SignWriting's integration into digital and computational systems. In educational contexts, studies have demonstrated that introducing SignWriting into early childhood education programs for Deaf learners can enhance metalinguistic awareness, support reading development in spoken language acquisition, and affirm the status of signed languages as complete linguistic systems worthy of literacy efforts (Fenlon *et al.,* 2015).

When examining writing systems across all languages, we consider the function each system serves and the level of linguistics it offers. Linguistics has various branches, each focusing on a distinct component of language. These branches collaborate to provide a thorough understanding of how language works, how it is constructed, how it changes, and how it is used in different circumstances (Genetti, C., & Adelman, 2019). These linguistic levels are: cherology, phonetics, phonology, morphonology, syntax, semantics, pragmatics, sociolinguistics, graphology, and orthography. There are significant differences in writing systems between spoken and signed languages. For example, at the most complex linguistic level, phonetics in spoken languages is defined as a branch of linguistics that deals with the study of speech sounds and how they are produced, transmitted, and perceived (Fasold & Connor-Lonton, 2006). International Phonetics Alphabets (IPA) is a system of phonetic transcription that uses a defined set of symbols to represent each unique sound (phoneme) in human speech, according to Crystal (2011). For example, when using the IPA, we can annotate the following words:

CAT: /kæt/,

DOG: [dɒg],

HOUSE: [haʊs].

Graphology is the study of a language's writing system, which is considered the least complicated linguistic level, simpler, and easier to use in everyday interactions. It includes the orthographic norms used to convert speech into writing using any available technology. The Roman/Latin alphabet is based on 26 letters, in both lower case (a, b, c...) and uppercase (A, B, C...) forms, along with spelling and capitalisation rules that regulate how these letters are combined to form words (Crystal, 2011). The Roman/Latin alphabet is used on an everyday basis and by many languages. Encyclopaedia Britannica (2024) states that the Roman/Latin alphabet is the most widely used alphabet writing system in the world, originally used by ancient Romans. The following English words are annotated using the Roman/Latin alphabet:

C-A-T: cat,

D-O-G: DOG,

H-O-U-S-E: house.

However, when it comes to sign languages, the SignWriting system can be used to write sign languages on multiple linguistic levels, including phonetic and graphology linguistic levels, depending on what you want to accomplish. sign phonetics is the study of how Ssign language is created and perceived. The creation and perception of a sign language can be affected by phrase structure, linguistic register, the signer's linguistic background, the visual perception mechanism, the anatomy and physiology of the hands and arms, and many other factors (Tyrone, 2020). The signs listed below are annotated using the Sutton SignWriting from the Centre for Sutton Movement Writing (n.d.):

CAT:

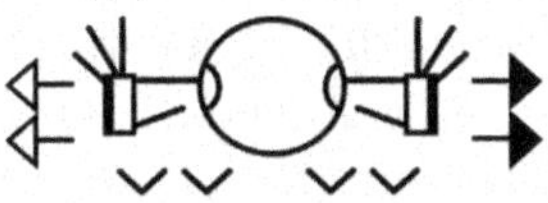

,

DOG:

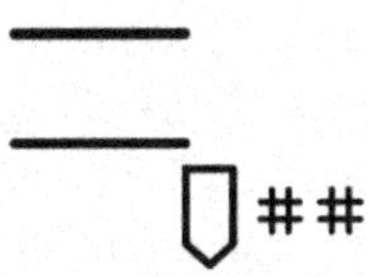

,

HOUSE:

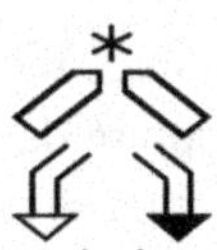

.

As a result, linguists, researchers, educators, and Deaf people can use this writing system. For instance, the Fulton School for the Deaf, based in Durban, Kwa-Zulu Natal, South Africa, implemented the SignWriting system into its teaching method. This initiative was led by their teacher Ingrid Foggitt, who notes:

"I believe that SW will give students (from preschool to high school) relaxed, interesting, exciting, and equal access to information. When I showed the few SW pages I had obtained from the Internet to my students, I ***knew*** *the introduction of SW would make a big difference to them, judging by their reactions and level of interest. SignWriting might also help in other subjects; for example, in science, students might like to make "margin notes" using SW to help them remember what a word/concept means" (Foggitt, I., 2000).*

While there is no available literature to confirm whether the Fulton School for the Deaf's initiative to implement SignWriting is still ongoing, it highlights the continued need for SignWriting within educational settings. The use of SignWriting can significantly contribute to the academic progress of Deaf students, providing them with a more effective means of communication and learning. In linguistic research, SignWriting has increasingly been adopted as a transcription system for creating detailed corpora of sign language use (Zwitserlood *et al.,* 2006). Projects documenting national and regional signed languages have begun to include SignWriting alongside video recordings and gloss annotations, using it to capture aspects of sign form and structure that are difficult to represent through glosses alone. Nonetheless, there remains considerable variation in how SignWriting is applied across different projects, reflecting methodological differences in transcription style, segmentation of sign units, and the granularity of phonological detail captured (Crasborn, 2018). It can also be argued that although SignWriting might be a viable system for capturing syntactic and semantic properties of a signed language, variation within sign languages might be reduced in text format. It is therefore vital to acknowledge that even though SignWriting as a viable text-based system is being advocated in this book, it is not a perfect solution to preserve a well-developed language and culture. Several efforts have been made to create machine-readable versions of SignWriting through encoding systems such as Formal SignWriting (Sutton & Frost, 2008) and Unicode-based standards (Slevin, 2010). Despite these efforts, challenges remain in standardising digital formats, ensuring interoperability between platforms, and addressing the complexity of representing three-dimensional movement in two-dimensional code (Hanke & Storz, 2008).

Another emerging field of research involves the automatic generation and recognition of SignWriting from video or motion capture data. Early prototypes have explored how computer vision systems could be trained to parse signing motion and automatically generate corresponding SignWriting outputs (Liwicki & Everingham, 2009). Conversely, projects have also investigated how SignWriting could serve as an intermediate representation for synthesising signing avatars or translating written signs back into animated forms (Krishna, 2021). However, these initiatives remain at early proof-of-concept stages, often constrained by limited datasets, variability in SignWriting transcription practices, and the inherent difficulty of modelling the simultaneity and multi-layered nature of signed communication (Lu & Huenerfauth, 2011).

From a sociolinguistic perspective, researchers have noted that the adoption of SignWriting is shaped by community attitudes toward the written forms of signed languages (Reagan, 2006). In many contexts, there is an ongoing debate about the desirability of developing a conventional written form for what has historically been a primarily oral-visual medium (Murray, 2015).

Collaborative projects have begun to explore the use of SignWriting across different signed languages, raising important questions about universality versus language-specific adaptations (Efthimiou *et al.,* 2012). While the basic symbols and conventions of SignWriting are designed to be flexible across different linguistic contexts, research has shown that adaptations are often necessary to accommodate the phonological, morphological, and syntactic particularities of each sign language. This has led to the development of language-specific SignWriting manuals, dictionaries, and teaching materials, further diversifying the research landscape (Fontana, 2008). Despite the growing interest, there remains a notable lack of longitudinal studies evaluating the long-term effects of SignWriting literacy on cognitive development, bilingual education outcomes, or sign language maintenance (Paludneviciene *et al.,* 2012). Most studies to date have been cross-sectional, small-scale, or anecdotal, leaving substantial gaps in understanding how the integration of SignWriting into educational systems and community practices might evolve over time. It is for these reasons that we argue SignWriting be an explicit written sign language system.

The transformation of SignWriting into human-like or schematic illustrations constitutes a complex and interdisciplinary challenge in the domain of sign language technology development. Illustrations derived from SignWriting are crucial to produce educational materials, the compilation of visual sign language dictionaries, the design of accessible language learning platforms, the promotion of literacy initiatives, and the enhancement of communication aids (Wilcox, 2000). Nevertheless, the process of moving from abstract, symbolic SignWriting notation to coherent and visually faithful human depictions raises profound linguistic, computational, artistic, and ethical issues that must be addressed carefully, particularly within the socio-cultural framework of SASL.

The symbolic abstraction of SignWriting underlies many of these challenges. Rather than aiming to replicate the human form anatomically, SignWriting uses a stylised two-dimensional system to encode the essential linguistic parameters of signing, such as handshapes, movements, palm orientations, and non-manual markers (Liddell, 2003). While this abstraction facilitates linguistic precision, it sacrifices anatomical realism and biomechanical information, thereby preventing a direct, unambiguous mapping from a SignWriting glyph to a full human pose. Producing illustrations from SignWriting thus demands inferential reasoning and interpretive synthesis rather than straightforward transcription, requiring models to reconstruct omitted details, resolve symbolic ambiguities, and generate plausible human poses (Leeson & Saeed, 2012).

Another fundamental difficulty stems from the compression of biomechanical, temporal, and spatial information within SignWriting scripts. Although key movement paths and orientations are captured, nuances such as the exact angles of elbow articulation, wrist flexibility, finger curvature dynamics, and transitional postures are generally absent (Emmorey, 2002). Similarly, important aspects of temporal motion, including the natural acceleration, deceleration, and rhythm of signing sequences, are abstracted into static spatial layouts. Generating convincing illustrations thus demands not only linguistic competence but also a sophisticated understanding of human kinematics and sign language embodiment principles (Cormier *et al.,* 2012).

Variation among SASL signers compounds this complexity. Signs are rarely produced identically across individuals; factors such as signer age, regional dialect, physical anatomy, signing style, and emotive expression introduce rich variation even within a single lexical item (de Beuzeville *et al.*, 2009). SignWriting captures a prototypical or canonical form, but real-world signing displays fluidity, subtlety, and adaptation to conversational context. Accordingly, illustration systems must balance the need for a clear, standardised form against the risk of flattening authentic linguistic diversity. Decision-making in this area must be informed by collaborative engagement with Deaf communities, linguists, and educators, ensuring that representations are inclusive, respectful, and culturally grounded (Wang & Napier, 2015).

The issue of cultural semiotics embedded in illustrations must also be recognised. Visual representations are not ideologically neutral; they convey implicit assumptions about language ownership, normative signing behaviour, and community identity (Turell, 2025). An illustration that unconsciously privileges a particular style, phenotype, or signing register risks alienating users whose identities and practices are not reflected. Systems that generate signing illustrations must therefore be carefully designed to avoid marginalisation and to embrace the full spectrum of sociolinguistic diversity present within SASL communities.

In conclusion, the task of generating illustrations from SignWriting for SASL is deeply interdisciplinary, intersecting fields such as sign linguistics, biomechanics, computer graphics, sociolinguistics, and Deaf Studies. It requires meticulous attention to linguistic accuracy, anatomical plausibility, cultural authenticity, and user-centric principles. While the path toward automated or semi-automated generation of such illustrations is fraught with complexity, achieving success would significantly enhance tools for Deaf education, literacy development, language documentation, and cultural representation, helping to affirm the visual-spatial brilliance and linguistic richness of SASL in a digital world.

4.4 Gaps in Achieving Optimal Illustrations for SASL: Influence of Demographics, Training Data, and Context

As research efforts advance toward the generation of static and dynamic illustrations from linguistic inputs such as SignWriting, gloss sequences, or pose estimations, it has become increasingly evident that no single method universally produces optimal illustrations for SASL users. Rather, the clarity, effectiveness, and cultural appropriateness of such outputs are profoundly influenced by a range of contextual variables, most notably demographic diversity, the characteristics of the training data, and the specific communicative or educational context in which the illustrations are deployed (Willcox, 2000). Recognising and addressing these contextual dependencies is crucial for avoiding oversimplified or exclusionary designs that fail to serve the needs of SASL communities adequately.

One primary challenge lies in achieving demographic sensitivity. South Africa's Deaf community encompasses a wide range of racial, ethnic, gender, age, regional, and educational backgrounds, each of which can influence signing styles, preferences for visual representation, and accessibility expectations (Morgan & Kaneko, 2017). Younger signers, particularly those immersed in digital cultures, may favour schematic, cartoon-like depictions that prioritise simplicity and accessibility. Conversely, older signers or those engaged in formal educational or linguistic settings may prefer more anatomically accurate, detailed visualisations that preserve the complexity of realistic handshapes, facial articulations, and bodily movements (Kurniawati *et al.,* 2021). Moreover, identity markers such as skin tone, facial structure, attire, and expressive style are not merely aesthetic considerations; they are central to authentic and inclusive representation (Leigh *et al.,* 2020). The capacity for demographic customisation must be a foundational design principle for SASL illustration technologies (Bauman & Murray, 2010).

The characteristics of training data further shape what models can produce. Existing visual datasets for sign language are often drawn from restricted environments, involving limited signer demographics, controlled backgrounds, and narrow linguistic registers (Crasborn, 2008). Consequently, models trained on such datasets tend to generate illustrations that lack the expressive richness and stylistic diversity characteristic of real-world SASL communication. Over-reliance on homogeneous datasets risks producing outputs that reinforce biases toward certain signing styles, movement types, or demographic profiles, thereby reducing representational accuracy and social inclusivity (Sandler *et al.,* 2019). Biases embedded within datasets, such as an overrepresentation of urban, academic signing styles, can systematically distort illustration outputs. For instance, if a model predominantly encounters young, urban signers during training, it may underrepresent rural variants of SASL, generational signing differences, or stylistic registers used in traditional storytelling and ceremonial contexts (Kahlon & Singh, 2023). Expanding training datasets to include diverse signer profiles, communicative genres, and sociolinguistic settings is thus essential for developing robust, contextually sensitive illustration models.

The context of use is another critical determinant of what constitutes "optimal" illustration. Different applications require varying levels of anatomical detail, stylistic abstraction, and linguistic precision. For example, in early childhood education, bright, exaggerated illustrations that simplify complex handshapes and facial grammar may improve engagement and comprehension (Marschark *et al.,* 2014). In adult literacy programs and formal sign language instruction, more anatomically faithful illustrations, with precise tracking of movement trajectories and non-manual grammatical markers, are necessary for effective language acquisition (Shand & Bowden, 2022). In scientific and technical documentation, illustrations must conform to standardised conventions to ensure linguistic and analytic consistency (Sutton-Spence, 2008). In public awareness campaigns or signage, highly recognisable and stylistically inclusive illustrations are preferred, even at the cost of minor linguistic oversimplifications (Napier & Leeson, 2016).

Failure to align illustration design with the communicative or pedagogical context risks reducing user comprehension, undermining trust in the material, or inadvertently excluding portions of the target audience. Systematic evaluation frameworks are urgently needed to assess illustration quality across different demographics, datasets, and contexts. Presently, evaluations often prioritise technical correctness, such as accurate depiction of handshape or orientation, but neglect deeper considerations of cultural resonance, user comprehension, and aesthetic engagement (Turner, 2009). Truly holistic evaluation protocols must involve diverse Deaf SASL users and must assess not only the linguistic fidelity of illustrations but also their communicative clarity, cultural appropriateness, and pedagogical effectiveness.

Achieving truly optimal illustrations for SASL demands a shift away from universalist, static approaches toward flexible, adaptive, and culturally sensitive design methodologies. For all these technologies to have an impact, rigorous engagement with the demographic diversity of SASL users, critical reflection on training data practices, context-aware application design, and user-centred evaluation protocols are required. Moving forward, interdisciplinary collaboration involving Deaf community leaders, linguists, educators, artists, technologists, and social scientists will be essential to ensure that illustration technologies not only serve communicative functions but also affirm and celebrate the full richness of the South African Deaf experience (Table 4.2).

Table 4.2: Challenges associated with SASL illustrations

Theme	Description
Demographic Sensitivity	Illustrations must reflect the racial, cultural, age, gender, and regional diversity of the Deaf community to ensure authentic, inclusive visual representations.
Training Data Limitations	Existing datasets are often small, homogenous, or laboratory-based, limiting models' ability to generalise to the variability and expressiveness of real-world SASL signing.

Theme	Description
Dataset Bias and Representational Gaps	Biases in training data can lead to systematic overrepresentation of certain signing styles or demographics, marginalising rural, traditional, or less-documented signing variants.
Context-Specific Illustration Requirements	Different communicative contexts, such as education, public awareness, or technical documentation, demand distinct levels of illustration detail, style, and linguistic precision.
Adaptive and Personalised Technologies	Future systems must dynamically adjust illustration style, complexity, and modality based on user profiles, interaction data, and specific accessibility needs.
Human-Centred Evaluation Frameworks	Assessment of illustrations must move beyond technical correctness to include cultural resonance, user comprehension, aesthetic appropriateness, and educational impact.

The requirements of different communicative contexts demand a nuanced, flexible approach to illustration generation, with application-specific standards guiding visual design choices. Emerging needs around adaptivity and personalisation also call for systems capable of dynamically responding to individual user profiles and preferences, enhancing engagement and comprehension. The field must advance beyond narrow technical evaluations, embracing human-centred frameworks that holistically assess linguistic accuracy, cultural authenticity, and communicative effectiveness. Together, these themes form a roadmap for future research and development efforts, ensuring that SASL illustration technologies evolve not only with technical precision but also with a profound commitment to inclusivity, accessibility, and cultural resonance. At the core of all technological advances lies the data, and the people who represent the data. Novel innovative ways of capturing, acquiring, sharing, and preserving the data is fundamentally needed.

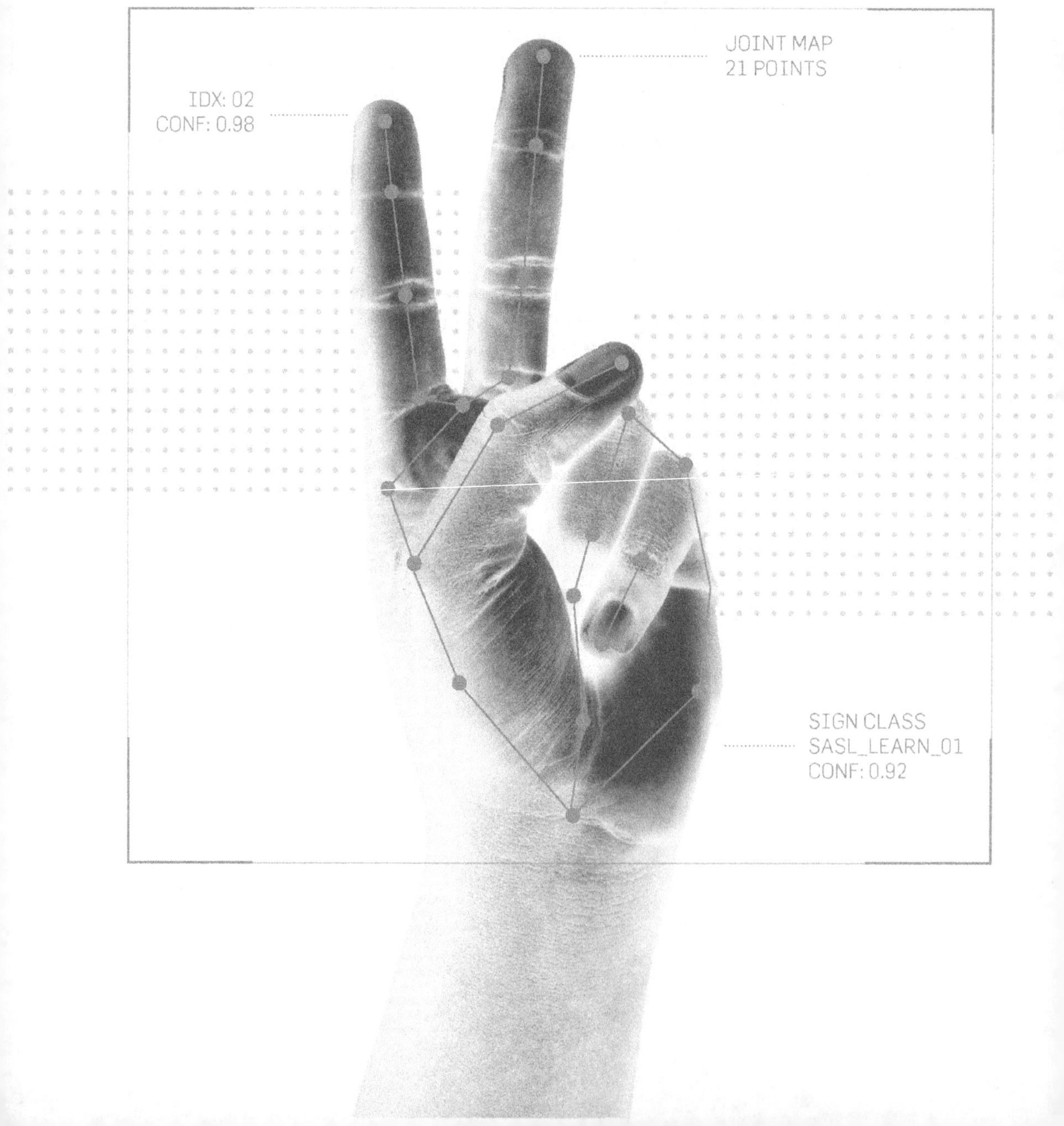
JOINT MAP
21 POINTS
IDX: 02
CONF: 0.98
SIGN CLASS
SASL_LEARN_01
CONF: 0.92

CHAPTER 5

Using Artificial Intelligence (AI) in Signed Languages

Dr. Herkulaas Combrink, Ms Charne Bornman, and Mr Nick Coetzee

The purpose of this chapter is to outline how artificial intelligence (AI) and machine learning (ML) is used in South African Sign Language (SASL). AI and ML are often used interchangeably, which is not entirely correct (Brown *et al.,* 2018). Technically, AI is a broad field that encompasses any technology that mimics human intelligence, while ML is a specific subset of AI algorithms that enable machines or computer-based systems to learn from data without explicit programming (James *et al.,* 2013; Brown *et al.,* 2018). This is taken even further by looking at deep learning, which applies ML algorithms within the context of neural networks comprising multiple hidden layers of processing (LeCun *et al.,* 2015).

5.1 ML in the Context of Supervised and Unsupervised Learning

ML, at its core, involves the development of algorithms that can learn from data to make predictions or decisions (James *et al.,*2013). ML can be subdivided into supervised and unsupervised learning algorithms. Deciding on what ML algorithm to use for research or data processing is typically based on what type of data you are working with (Brown *et al.,* 2018). In the context of data science and information systems, understanding the classification of data types is fundamental for selecting appropriate processing, storage, and analysis techniques. Information in this context is typically categorised into four broad types: structured, unstructured, semi-structured, and metadata, each with distinct characteristics and implications for computational handling. Structured data refers to information that conforms to a fixed schema or model, making it highly organised and easily searchable within relational databases (Elmasri & Navathe, 2015). Typically presented in tabular formats, structured data consists of clearly defined fields such as names, dates, credit card numbers, or stock information. In the context of SASL, these will be words associated with their respective signs, with additional computer-readable data. In contrast, unstructured data lacks a predefined format or consistent model, presenting significant challenges for automated processing and analysis (Gandomi & Haider, 2015).

This category includes diverse content forms such as sensor outputs, emails, social media posts, blog entries, word processing files, PDFs, and images. In the context of SASL, this is in the form of SASL dialogues, video content, and largely, the visual training data upon which ML models are trained. Although rich in informational content, the inherent variability and complexity of unstructured data necessitate advanced analytical approaches, including natural language processing, computer vision, and ML algorithms.

Semi-structured data occupies an intermediate position between structured and unstructured forms, which possess inherent organisational properties, such as hierarchical tags or key-value pairs, that facilitate its interpretation (Abiteboul, 1997). Metadata plays a crucial role in enhancing the usability and contextual understanding of other data types. Defined as "data about data", metadata provides descriptive, structural, or administrative information regarding a resource (Baca, 2016). Typical examples include the author of a document, file size, creation date, and associated keywords. Metadata is pivotal in data governance, indexing, discovery, and interoperability, enabling users and systems to organise, retrieve, and manage information more effectively (Table 5.1).

Table 5.1: Summary of different data types

Type	Definition	Examples
Structured Data	Data with a well-defined structure conforms to a data model, is stored in a standard format (usually tabular), easily accessed and used by programs.	Names, dates, addresses, credit card numbers, stock information, geolocation, etc.
Unstructured Data	Data without a predefined format or organisation; difficult to capture, process, and analyse; often includes text and multimedia.	Sensor data, emails, blog entries, wikis, word processing documents, PDF files, audio, videos, images, presentations, web pages, etc.
Semi-structured Data	Data not stored in traditional relational databases but has some organisational properties that make it easier to analyse than unstructured data.	HTML, XML, JSON, NoSQL databases, etc.
Metadata	Data about data; provides information that describes, defines, or explains other data to give it more meaning and context.	Author, file size, date created, keywords of a document, etc.

Supervised learning is a foundational approach within ML that utilises labelled datasets, where the correct output is known for each corresponding input, to train predictive models (Brown *et al.,* 2018). In supervised learning, the algorithm is exposed to a set of training examples in which each instance is explicitly paired with its target outcome. Through this process, the model infers the underlying relationships between inputs and outputs, enabling it to generalise and make accurate predictions or classifications when presented with novel, unseen data. For instance, within a healthcare setting, a supervised model may be trained on historical patient records containing symptom profiles and confirmed medical diagnoses.

Once trained, the model can predict the probable diagnosis for new patients based on their reported symptoms. Supervised learning is particularly well-suited for classification tasks, where inputs are assigned to predefined discrete categories, and for regression tasks, which involve predicting continuous numerical values. The availability of explicit labels during training offers a clear framework for the algorithm to optimise its predictive performance, facilitating robust outcomes in a range of applications.

Conversely, unsupervised learning operates on datasets that lack explicit labels, requiring the algorithm to autonomously detect patterns, structures, or intrinsic relationships within the data (Ghosh *et al.,* 2019). Without labelled outputs to guide learning, unsupervised algorithms seek to uncover hidden structures that may not be immediately apparent. A common application of this approach is clustering, wherein a model identifies natural groupings of data points based on their similarities.

For example, in a commercial context, an unsupervised algorithm may analyse customer purchasing behaviours without prior categorisation and segment the customers into distinct behavioural groups. Such capabilities make unsupervised learning particularly valuable for exploratory data analysis, especially in complex domains where the data's inherent structure is unknown or poorly understood, including raw video, audio files, and textual corpora (Hilton *et al.,* 2006). Through these methods, unsupervised learning enables the discovery of meaningful insights from unlabelled and often unstructured datasets, expanding the potential for knowledge extraction beyond the limitations of supervised frameworks. It is useful to think about ML from the perspective of the task that the model is trying to execute, and the first type of model that will be outlined is a classification-based task.

5.2 ML Classification Tasks

Imagine a file on a computer containing hundreds of different signs for SASL in the folder, each sign representing a different word, and you are trying to sort all these SASL words into groups or folders depending on where they belong. Some signs are static, like letters in the alphabet, some are based on movement, and some are a combination of complex signs. To do this, you would need to examine the signs to determine which belongs to which category, and then decide which folder to place it in. By going through the dataset, you will learn that static signs are represented by images, while signs that move are represented by videos. A classification algorithm does the same thing with data, learning from labelled examples to sort new items into the correct groups (Sen *et al.,* 2020). This process is a key part of supervised learning, in which the computer relies on a "teacher" (data with labels like the sign for "I love you" or the sign for the letter "S") to discover patterns and make predictions about new, unlabelled data (Hastie *et al.,* 2009).

Classification tasks are a cornerstone of AI, powering applications from spotting spam emails to helping doctors diagnose illnesses (Oza &Tumer, 2008). This classification process falls under supervised learning because it depends on labelled data to guide the computer's learning, much like a student learning from a textbook with answers in the back. For example, to teach a computer to identify a specific set of signs, you would give it a dataset of those signs already marked as the letters you want the system to identify. The computer studies feature (or variables) of these signs, for example, certain movements or hand positions, to learn what makes those letters unique. This type of task is used in a variety of applications, including, for example, email spam identification (Roy & Viswanatham, 2016). Once trained, the algorithm can predict those patterns, and the task of those developing the system is to ensure that the models are accurate enough and have minimal bias within the outcome. Although not perfect, these supervised approaches make classification practical for real-world tasks, particularly when the tasks performed are trained on data with the same patterns. However, they require a lot of labelled data, which can be time-consuming to gather.

The power of classification lies in its ability to automate decisions that would otherwise require human expertise, save time, and boost efficiency. In sign language production, classifications can analyse SASL dialogue to detect if a person is finger spelling or contributing to the dialogue (Oza & Tumer, 2008). Classification tasks can also flag unique signs that are being discussed for the first time, such as variations that occur for the same place name. These examples show how versatile classification is, but they also highlight a limitation: a classification model requires high-quality data and the right algorithms to work well. If the information is messy and underlying data unstructured or biased, for example, if it only includes examples from one group, the computer may make mistakes or unfair predictions, such as misclassifying legitimate transactions as fraud. Classification tasks vary widely, and in the context of SASL, understanding these differences helps us understand how they are currently applied and how they may be applied in future. Binary classification, the simplest form, sorts data into two distinct groups, such as determining whether a person is fingerspelling at a specific time step or not (Sen *et al.,* 2020).

Multiclass classification, on the other hand, increases in complexity, sorting data into more than two groups, with each item belonging to exactly one (Sen *et al.,* 2020). Imagine a dialogue in SASL where there is a need to identify the place name being discussed. The computer learns the unique features of each hand sign for a specific place and considers all the variations of that place but should also ensure that the conversation is about a place name and not a person's name, when making the classification to make the call (Iancu *et al.,* 2019). This is common in image recognition, such as classifying what the next SASL word or context might be (Foody & Mathur, 2004). Multilabel classification is more flexible, allowing a single item to belong to multiple groups simultaneously (Sen *et al.,* 2020; Bogatinovski *et al.,* 2022).

Imbalanced classification tackles a common real-world problem, such as imbalanced datasets. In the detection of rare words in SASL, for instance, like a place name, the place name occurs less frequently than a noun or verb in conversation, making it hard for the computer to learn what a SASL place name is. Special techniques, like oversampling the rare cases or adjusting the algorithm to pay more attention to them, help balance things out (Spelmen & Porkodi, 2018). An illustration of the three types of classifiers can be seen in Figure 5.1.

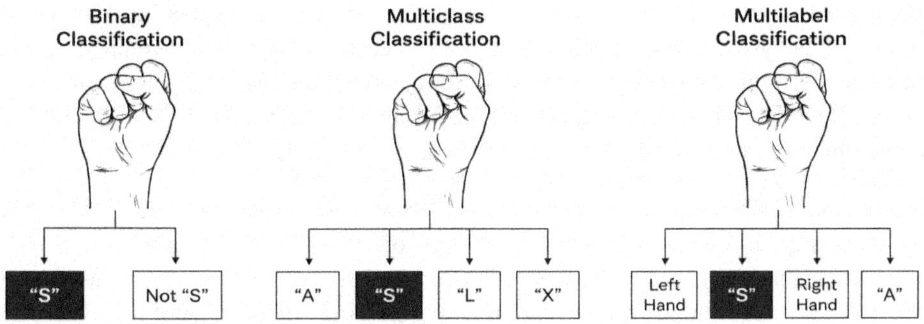

***Figure 5.1**: Types of classification tasks.*

Figure 5.1 illustrates three types of ML classification using a picture of a hand sign representing the SASL letter "S." In binary classification, the task is to categorise the sign into one of two classes, such as "S" or "Not S," determining simply whether the sign is the letter "S." Multiclass classification expands this to multiple exclusive categories, such as "A," "S," "L," or "X," where the sign is assigned as one category/letter, "S." In contrast, multilabel classification identifies more than one applicable class. In this case, both the letter and the hand used are identified, so the sign is tagged as "S" (the letter) and "Right Hand" (the hand used), indicating that it is the letter "S" made with the right hand. The "Left Hand" and "A" labels are alternatives that would be chosen if the sign were made with the left hand or represented the letter "A" instead.

Each type of classification has its own challenges, but they all rely on the same core idea: learning from examples to make a prediction, given the parameters of the model. The choice of algorithm can make a big difference in how well this works, as well as the choice of parameters and, most importantly, the underlying data. Behind the scenes, classification algorithms use different strategies to sort data, each with its own way of tackling the problem. Some, like logistic regression, draw a line to separate groups, while others, like decision trees, ask a series of questions to narrow down the options. More advanced methods, like random forests, combine multiple approaches for better accuracy. Choosing the right algorithm depends on the task, the data, and whether you need the results to be easy to explain or extremely precise.

5.3 Common Classification Algorithms

5.3.1 Support Vector Machines (SVM)

Support Vector Machines (SVM) are a method to classify data points by finding the best boundary to separate groups or classes. Figure 2 shows how SVM works by drawing a line to separate two SASL signs, "A" (Class 2) and "S" (Class 1), based on hand compactness (x-axis) and thumb angle (y-axis). Signs for "A" are grouped in the upper-left with a higher thumb angle, around 90° (thumb extended upward), and a less compact hand, while "S" signs are in the lower-right with a lower thumb angle, around 0° (thumb wrapped over the fingers), and a more compact hand. SVM places a hyperplane diagonally across the graph to divide the two groups, ensuring the widest possible space, called the margin, between the hyperplane and the closest "A" and "S" signs on each side.

In this example, the task of the algorithm is to decide, whether you provide the algorithm with a new sign, if the sign forms part of the "S" or the "A". This margin, shown by the dashed lines (Figure 2), makes the separation distinct, so even if a new sign varies slightly in the variables associated with the sign, it is still classified on the side of the hyperplane based on what has been learned. SVM is great for complex tasks like image classification or text analysis, but it can struggle with noisy data and needs careful tweaking to work at its best (Foody and Mathur, 2004).

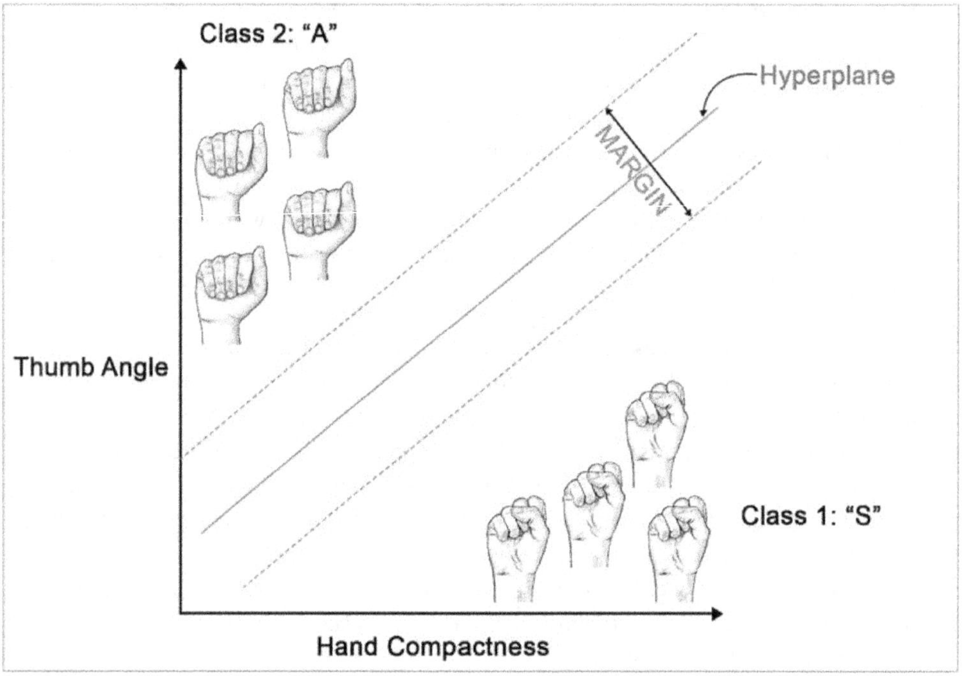

***Figure 5.2**: Example of Support Vector Machines in SASL.*

However, if the data to train the model does not include a balanced representation of a specific sign, then the model will not learn what that sign means and would thus be excluded from the model. As with all ML, a lot of training data is used to build a model. If the underlying information is therefore not of a good quality or a large enough sample size, then the model will fail to perform the desired output for the task. Therefore, a great deal of time is spent on the conceptualisation, design, and development of such systems. Another important algorithm used for classification tasks is the K-Nearest Neighbour (KNN) algorithm.

5.3.2 K-Nearest Neighbours (KNN)

KNN is a non-parametric algorithm that works by plotting data in a feature space and casting a vote to determine the most optimal outcome based on a certain set of variables. When there is new data to classify, KNN examines the closest examples in the training data, and validates their labels based on the number of votes, or closest neighbours, based on what the model has learned (Mucherino, Papajorgji & Pardalos, 2009). It's a majority vote based on similarity, measured by distance, like how close two points are on a map. The number of votes is determined by the value of K. For example, if K is set as 7, then the model will look at the 7 closest points in the feature space to determine where the new data point belongs to the nearest neighbours by distance. Suppose we trained a model that can identify two signs, an "A" and "S", and we introduce a new sign which is an "S" but with left-hand orientation instead of right-hand orientation (Figure 5.3).

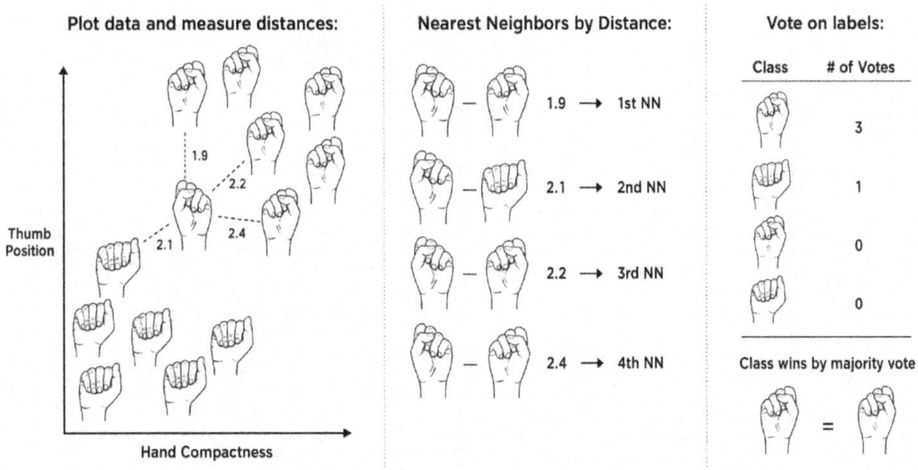

Figure 5.3*: Example of K-Nearest Neighbour algorithm for SASL.*

The first step is to plot the data on a graph and let us suppose that we are only measuring the variables "Hand Compactness" (x-axis) and "Thumb Position" (y-axis). Signs for "A" (thumb extended, higher position) are shown in one cluster, and signs for "S" (thumb wrapped, lower position) in another, both depicted as hand icons. A new sign, an "S" made with the left hand, needs classification, and distances are calculated to all others, with the closest marked (e.g., 1.9, 2.1, 2.2, 2.4).

The step ranks these neighbours based on their nearest neighbour by distance. In other words, how close is the sign to the different data points within the already existing model? In this example, the first neighbour at 1.9 units is labelled as an "S" sign, the second at 2.1 units as an "A" sign, the third at 2.2 units as an "S" sign, and the fourth at 2.4 units as an "S" sign. The final step determines the voting process using the four nearest neighbours (K=4). In this example, three neighbours voted the left-handed sign as the "S" sign, and one neighbour voted the left-handed sign as an "A" sign. Therefore, the left-handed sign will be classified as an "S" sign in this model based on the majority vote, which means that KNN classifies the new left-handed sign as "S". KNN is simple and intuitive, making it great for tasks like pattern recognition or recommendation systems, but it can be slow with large datasets because it must compare the new data to every example (Mucherino *et al.,* 2009; Steinbach & Tan, 2009). It is also sensitive to outliers that can throw off the vote (Steinbach & Tan, 2009). Another useful type of classifier that has utility in deep learning is logistic regression.

5.3.3 Logistic Regression

Logistic regression is an algorithm that classifies data depending on the properties of a sigmoid function and a probability threshold (Hosmer *et al.,* 2013). In other words, let us determine the likelihood of a sign being the letter "A" or the letter "S" based on a threshold. Logistic regression calculates a probability, such as a 70% chance of the new sign being an "A", and if it is above a certain cut-off (usually 50%), it says "A" (Figure 5.4).

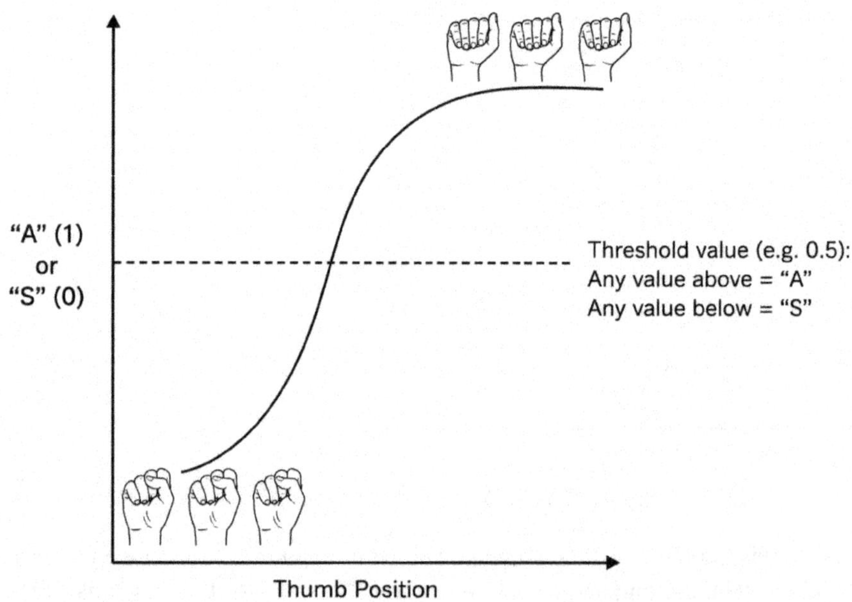

***Figure 5.4**: Example Logistic Regression in SASL classification.*

Figure 5.4 illustrates how logistic regression classifies South SASL based on an S curve that maps thumb position to this probability, 0 for not the "S" signs and rising to 1 for the

"S" sign. A dashed threshold line at 0.5 on the y-axis determines the classification: signs with a probability above 0.5 (higher thumb position values) are classified as "S", while those below 0.5 (lower thumb position values) are classified as not "S", which in this case may represent the "A" sign.

Logistic regression is often used for two-category problems, like yes or no, but can handle more categories with some adaptation (Friedman *et al.,* 2000). Logistic regression is easy to understand and works well when the data can be separated by a straight line, making it popular for tasks that have two outcomes in the classification (Sultana *et al.,* 2018; Kontsewaya *et al.,* 2021). The final algorithm that we will outline is a decision tree algorithm. Decision trees work by dividing the data into smaller subsets. Each of these subsets of data undergoes a smaller learning task with less information, and thus the algorithm learns patterns present within each subset with some characteristics about the smaller subset. Then, once enough learning has taken place, the possible number of outcomes are decided based on a vote for categorical data or an average in the case of data that uses variables that are continuous.

Imagine a game of 20 Questions, where each question narrows down the possibilities until you reach an answer. For example, to classify a hand sign, a decision tree might split the data to determine a small characteristic about the overall hand sign, like the thumb position, and another subset, like index finger position, palm orientation, and so on. Then, these smaller trained patterns will be linked to the overall task of the algorithm, like is this an 'A' sign or an 'S' sign"? Decision trees are easy to understand because you can visualise them as a flowchart, and they work with all kinds of data. But they can sometimes get too specific, memorising the training data instead of learning general patterns, a problem called overfitting. The type of decision tree is largely determined by how the data splitting takes place, and a widely known and used decision tree is a random forest algorithm (Rincy & Gupta, 2020).

5.3.4 Random Forest

Random forest is like assembling a team of experts, each with a slightly different perspective, to vote on a decision. Each expert is a decision tree, a flowchart that asks questions about the data in order to reach a category (Bernard *et al.,* 2009). Random forest builds many of these trees, each trained on a random chunk of the data, so they don't all make the same mistakes (Bernard *et al.,* 2009; Parmar *et al.,* 2019). Figure 5.5 demonstrates how random forest classification works to identify an SASL sign; here, the letter "A".

In this diagram, three trees are shown, and each tree evaluates the sign based on different variables (such as thumb position or hand compactness from previous examples) through a series of yes/no questions, represented by nodes and branches, leading to a classification at the leaves. Tree 1 and Tree 2 both classify the sign as "A", while Tree 3 classifies it as "S". The predictions from all trees are then combined through majority voting, shown in the blue box at the bottom. With two votes for "A" and one for "S", the majority vote determines the final classification as "A" accurately identifying the sign in the image.

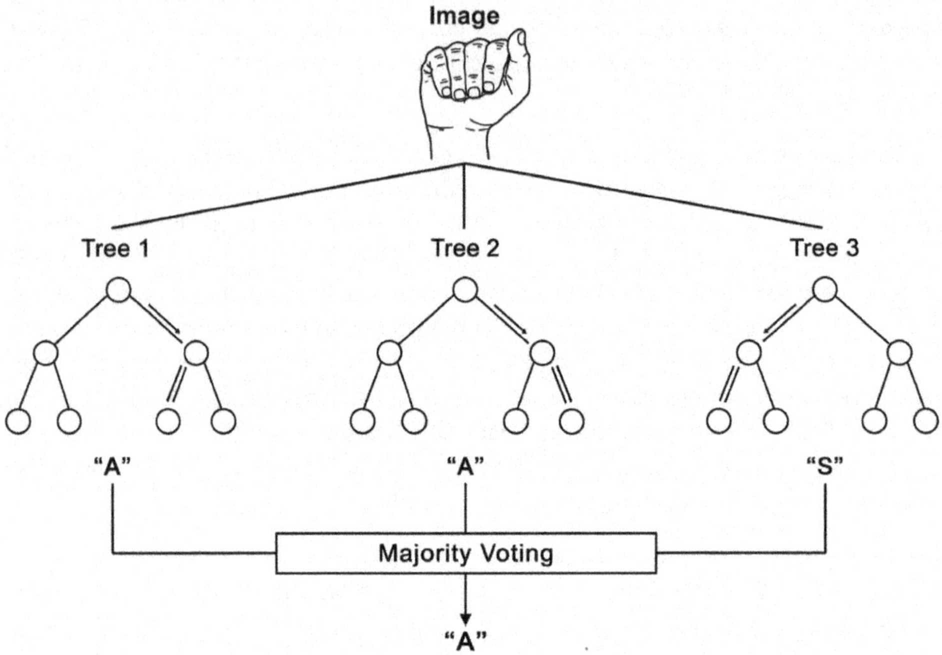

***Figure 5.5**: Example of Random Forest algorithm for SASL classification.*

Splitting data and making complex decisions on subsets of the data allows for classifications of the complex and noisy data as demonstrated by some studies (Liu *et al.,* 2015; Kumar *et al.,* 2019; Wang *et al.,* 2024). For example, XGBoost is a popular version of boosting that is fast and powerful, often used in competitions and real-world tasks like predicting customer behaviour or detecting diseases (Mateo *et al.,* 2021; Xu, 2024). It's great at handling complex data but can be tricky to set up, needing careful adjustments to get the best results (Bentéjac, Csörgő and Martínez-Muñoz, 2021).

Naive Bayes is another decision tree that has been used to calculate the probability an email is spam based on how often those words appear in spam versus non-spam emails and picks the most likely category (Zhang & Li, 2007; Sammut & Webb, 2011; Wei, 2018). It is called "naive" because of this assumption, but it is surprisingly effective, especially for text data like emails or social media posts and does so with relatively low resources (Gurkhe *et al.,* 2014). However, ML classifiers can struggle if the features are related, limiting their use for more complex tasks (Rish, 2001). To mitigate this, deep learning is a viable solution.

5.4 Deep Learning

Deep learning is a subfield of ML capable of handling complex, high-dimensional data challenges. Depending on the design, deep learning models can autonomously learn feature representations directly from raw input data (Deng & Yu, 2014). At its foundation, deep learning relies on artificial neural networks comprising multiple layers of interconnected computational units, loosely inspired by the organisation of biological neurons in the human brain (Schmidhuber, 2014). Each unit processes information received from preceding layers, applies a non-linear transformation, and transmits the result forward.

These layers process sub-classes of information from the original input to extract often missed patterns by traditional ML. It must be noted that deep learning is not better or worse than ML but rather has a specific function depending on the underlying data and the task it is trying to perform. In the context of a sign language, specifically hand recognition, early layers in the deep learning network typically detect elementary features such as edges or textures, while successive layers integrate these features into complex objects, activities, or linguistic constructs (Kothadiya *et al.*, 2022; Bengio *et al.*, 2013).

One of the key advantages of deep learning is its ability to perform end-to-end learning, integrating feature extraction, feature selection, and predictive modelling into a unified framework. Traditional ML pipelines typically require distinct stages for each of these tasks, often relying on substantial domain expertise (Jordan & Mitchell, 2015). In contrast, deep learning models can self-optimise internal representations during training, resulting in greater efficiency and adaptability across diverse and complex data environments.

Nonetheless, the power of deep learning models comes with significant demands for large, labelled datasets. The vast number of parameters that deep networks must learn necessitates extensive exposure to data to ensure generalisation and to prevent overfitting (Zhu, 2005). This data-intensive nature has historically limited the application of deep learning, but has been mitigated by advances in computational hardware, particularly graphics processing units (GPUs), which have enabled scalable training of extremely large models (Raina *et al.,* 2009). In other words, with advances in computational processing, deep learning has become more widely accessible and used in everyday tasks. Research in deep learning has expanded to all domains and is a very important innovation in technological advancement (Zhen & Yao, 2021).

Sign language human language technology comprises a variety of sub-interdisciplinary fields, including natural language processing and computer vision. Convolutional neural networks (CNNs) are used in computer vision tasks, specifically for image recognition, object detection, and semantic segmentation (Simonyan & Zisserman, 2015). For sequential data, like time series data or capturing the temporal sequence within sign languages, recurrent neural networks (RNNs) have become essential (Arun Prasath & Annapurani, 2023; Graves, 2013). Meanwhile, generative adversarial networks (GANs) have opened new research specifically in the generation of synthetic yet highly realistic data for artificial intelligence (Rahman *et al.,* 2024; Radford *et al.,* 2016). SASL technology includes the detection, analysis, and synthetic creation of handshapes, movements, and spatial locations during a conversation, among other language technology tasks (Figure 5.6).

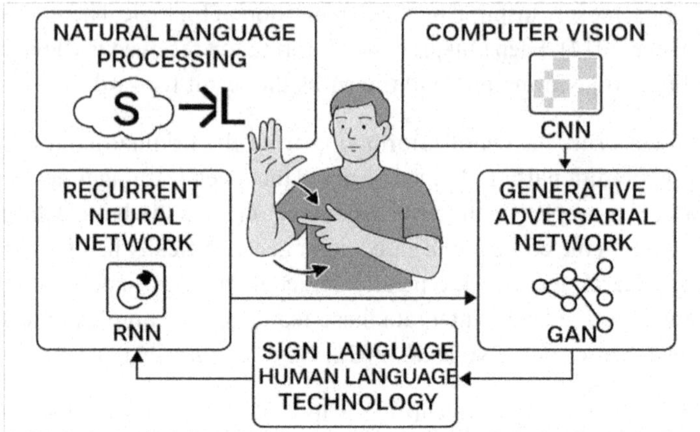

Figure 5.6: *AI in Sign Language technology.*

Additionally, elements such as Signwriting also use these technologies within human language technology (Buttar *et al.,* 2023; Koller, 2020). SASL is under-represented in terms of the amount of available training data for human language technology development (Thangaraj *et al.,* 2024; Marivate *et al.,* 2023). As a result, GANS have been used to generate synthetic sign language data (Natarajan & Elakkiya, 2022; Joze & Koller, 2019).

Deep learning has also demonstrated transformative potential in sign language translation tasks, where the objective is to map sequences of signs into coherent spoken or written language outputs. Encoder-decoder architectures, initially designed for machine translation between spoken languages, have been adapted for sign language translation by encoding video sequences into intermediate feature representations and decoding them into grammatically accurate textual output (Alam *et al.,* 2024). These models enable the construction of end-to-end translation systems capable of handling the intricate morphosyntactic structures and simultaneous articulations characteristic of signed communication. As mentioned, prior, however, all of these advances are predominantly focused on hearing-specific human language technologies, and not Deaf specific ones (Figure 5.7).

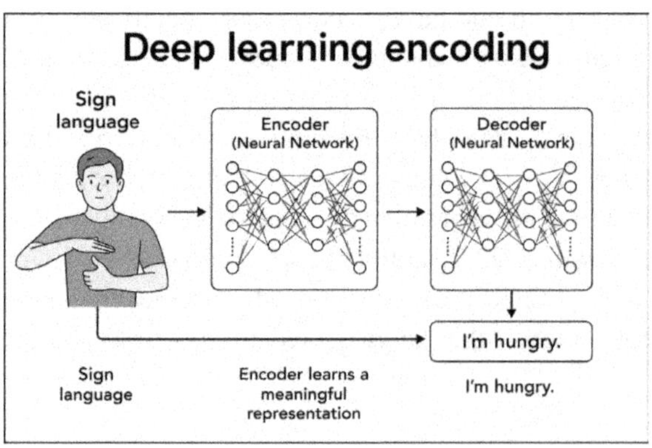

Figure 5.7: *Deep learning encoding.*

Despite its powerful contributions, deep learning in sign language processing is not without limitations. Deep neural networks are heavily reliant on large volumes of annotated data for effective training, which presents challenges in the context of sign languages, where labelled corpora are scarce and labour-intensive to create (Anderson *et al.,* 2017). Computational demands are also considerable, with training and fine-tuning requiring substantial hardware resources (Doshi-Velez & Kim, 2017). Risks of overfitting are particularly acute in sign language datasets due to limited sample diversity, and biases in training data may propagate into model outputs, raising ethical concerns around fairness, inclusivity, and representation (Ntoutsi *et al.,* 2020).

Nevertheless, the application of deep learning techniques represents a significant step forward in advancing sign language technology. Unlike rigid, rule-based systems, deep learning models offer flexibility and adaptability, better accommodating the natural variability and dynamism of human signing behaviour. As computational resources continue to expand and as community-driven efforts lead to the growth of annotated SASL datasets, deep learning is poised to play an increasingly central role in developing accurate, accessible, and culturally attuned sign language processing systems.

A major advantage of deep learning, such as RNNs and CNNs, lies in their inherent ability to preserve spatial hierarchies within the data. Through architectural components such as pooling layers, which summarise local neighbourhoods of features, CNNs maintain critical information regarding the relative spatial positioning of visual elements (Springenberg *et al.,* 2014).

This capacity is essential for sign language recognition, where semantic distinctions frequently hinge not solely on the presence of specific articulators but also on their spatial orientation and movement through the signing space. Thus, deep learning provides a powerful computational framework for capturing the multi-level, spatially dynamic visual features fundamental to the successful interpretation of sign language communication. Their integration into sign language human language technology represents a critical step toward developing more accurate, scalable, and culturally responsive language technologies for Deaf communities. As the field matures, it will be essential to harness the strengths of deep learning while navigating its challenges with care, ensuring that synthetic data generation enhances the linguistic authenticity, cultural dignity, and community empowerment that must remain at the heart of all SASL human language technology initiatives.

The strength of deep learning lies not only in the power of individual architectures but also in the flexible and dynamic integration of different technologies to solve complex, multifaceted problems. In advanced ML systems, it is increasingly common to build composite architectures that combine the unique strengths of a combination of ML and multiple deep learning models into unified, synergistic pipelines for very specific tasks. Understanding how these models work together, and more broadly how deep learning frameworks integrate diverse technologies, is critical for appreciating the state-of-the-art developments in SASL human language technology research and application.

Beyond this immediate integration, deep learning systems often architect broader hybrid models that bring together multiple specialised components to handle the full complexity of sign language processing. Importantly, the successful integration of multiple deep learning technologies requires careful system design, enough good training data, the skills to perform these tasks, and a research agenda that may streamline the research innovations in this domain. Models must be developed with attention to compatibility, training stability, computational efficiency, interpretability, and, most importantly, Deaf and hearing scientists working together to solve these problems.

In the specific case of SASL, where the sociolinguistic landscape is rich and varied, and where annotated datasets remain relatively scarce, the integrated use of deep learning technologies offers a powerful and necessary pathway forward. These integrated systems can bridge resource gaps, enhance the inclusivity of models across different SASL dialects and signing communities, and enable the development of advanced applications that focus on relevant innovations. The integration of multiple technologies in deep learning reflects a paradigm shift toward building comprehensive, resilient, and inclusive systems capable of capturing the full richness of human communication, a vision that is especially vital for the future of sign language technologies. For this to work, a dedicated research agenda needs to be established.

CHAPTER 6

Licensing Agreements Related to SASL Data

Dr. Herkulaas Combrink

6.1 Introduction

The purpose of this chapter is to discuss a licencing agreement that can benefit the sharing of data for human language technologies. Collaboration relies on the transfer of knowledge, and data sharing is a fundamental construct of that. For South African Sign Language (SASL), human language technologies rely fundamentally on the ways that we can share SASL-specific datasets between researchers and institutions (Combrink *et al.,* 2023). This is particularly critical in the context of training data used to develop SASL-based artificial intelligence (AI), machine learning (ML), deep learning, natural language processing, and other AI systems. As these technologies increasingly intersect with the domain of linguistics and sociocultural research, safeguarding the intellectual rights, cultural heritage, and labour contributions of marginalised language communities has become a pressing ethical imperative (Bird, 2020; Grenoble & Singerman, 2014).

SASL, as a historically marginalised language, faces heightened risks of technological exclusion and data appropriation. Without explicit protective measures, there is a substantial danger that the linguistic data and intellectual labour provided by Deaf communities could be exploited, commodified, misappropriated, or rendered inaccessible to the very groups for whom the technologies are designed (Boyles & Talbot, 2017). These risks are amplified in a rapidly commercialising AI ecosystem where proprietary models often eclipse principles of equitable knowledge sharing and cultural respect (Benjamin, 2023; Bragg *et al.,* 2020).

The mechanisms that allow free and open research, which maintain economic value from innovations built for these communities, ensure sustainability in the innovation landscape related to SASL human language technologies. Licensing agreements directly shape who can access SASL datasets, under what terms, for which purposes, and with what obligations to the originating community (Dunleavy & Margetts, 2025).

6.2 Background: The Linguistic and Technological Context of SASL

The integration of SASL into AI-powered systems holds great promise for improving accessibility, education, and cultural representation (Marschark *et al.,* 2014; Efthimiou *et al.,* 2012). However, these developments also introduce pathways for exploitative data extraction and enclosure. In response to these challenges, the licensing framework proposed for SASL human language technologies is rooted in principles of open collaboration, ethical AI development, and community-centred data governance (Combrink *et al.,* 2025).

The adoption of the Creative Commons Attribution-Non-Commercial-Share Alike (CC BY-NC-SA) licence model reflects a commitment to inclusive research practices. This licence allows for broad academic, educational, and non-profit use, while explicitly prohibiting unauthorised commercial use and mandating the openness of derivative works. The key here is that commercialisation is still welcomed, but it needs to be authorised. Such a framework aligns with recent calls for equitable data governance in AI and natural language processing, especially when working with under-represented linguistic communities (Tomalin *et al.,* 2021; Chelliah & de Reuse, 2010; Leavy *et al.,* 2020; Hummel *et al.,* 2021).

Data stewardship ensures ethical accountability, ownership, and sustained benefit for marginalised communities, including the various Deaf communities whose primary mode of communication is SASL (Klein *et al.,* 2024; McLester-Davis *et al.,* 2023). Through SASL datasets and technologies, the future of digital innovation can be redirected toward enhancing, rather than exploiting, the linguistic and cultural heritage of South African Deaf communities.

SASL occupies a unique and complex position within the national linguistic landscape and the global field of human language technology (Batterbury, 2012). Unlike spoken languages, SASL lacks a standardised orthographic form, complicating the application of traditional natural language processing methods. Within Deaf communities, standardisation of SASL is not part of the agenda to advance the language; instead, local variation persists within different South African Deaf communities. This variation means that each community will ultimately have nuanced and different signs for certain words, making human language technological development interesting, complex, and contextual (Al-Qurishi *et al.,* 2021). Therefore, the collection, annotation, and curation of representative datasets require not only technical expertise, but also profound cultural and linguistic sensitivity (Fenlon *et al.,* 2015; Efthimiou *et al.,* 2012).

The growing emergence of sign language technologies, including sign language corpora, holds immense potential for advancing Deaf education, social inclusion, and information access (Bragg *et al.,* 2020). The scarcity and high production cost of well-annotated SASL datasets make them attractive targets for exploitation, particularly by commercial actors seeking to capitalise on under-resourced language technologies without offering reciprocal benefit to the communities that generated the data (Tomalin *et al.,* 2021). It must be noted that research is important, and research costs money to perform. An oversight from researchers in performing research on specific communities is not to close the feedback loop when working with a specific community of people. In other words, when a researcher or researchers perform work with specific communities, like Deaf communities, and data collection, etc. takes place, the researchers should return to those communities to perform the research.

There is a real and urgent threat that datasets created through the labour of researchers, linguists, and community members could be extracted, refined, and reissued under restrictive proprietary licences that exclude the very users the technologies are intended to serve (McLester-Davis *et al.,* 2023; Dunleavy & Margetts, 2025). Recent research highlights how the absence of clearly defined licensing instruments has enabled private entities to extract open-access linguistic datasets, refine them through proprietary processes, and restrict re-use via closed models. In this example, when models are built, the training data for these models are often not disclosed; and thus, the use of the community information is not known. This effectively excludes the acknowledgement of the very communities from which the data originated (Hechler *et al.,* 2020; Okorie & Marivate, 2024). Consequently, datasets derived from SASL communication are not merely technical inputs but representations of lived experience (GPAI, 2022; Takyi *et al.,* 2025).

Licensing decisions cannot be separated from the broader context of digital colonialism. Scholars have increasingly observed that data extracted from low resource is often recontextualised within commercial systems that limit downstream accessibility and remove community oversight (Tomalin *et al.,* 2021; Klein *et al.,* 2024). In the case of SASL, the risk of community oversight is exacerbated by a lack of institutional mechanisms that would otherwise enable Deaf stakeholders to meaningfully participate in the governance of their own linguistic data. The intensification of global interest in sign language datasets, driven by advancements in ML and computer vision, will therefore introduce further complications.

Commercial actors, particularly those operating outside of South Africa, may treat SASL corpora as raw material for system training without engaging with the epistemic and ethical contexts in which the language is used. Without structured, enforceable licensing schemes, these practices risk normalising extractive models of technological development that are misaligned with the values and priorities of Deaf communities (Li & Chignell, 2022; Bragg *et al.,* 2020). SASL data cannot be approached as a generic linguistic asset. Rather, it should be understood as a form of community-embedded knowledge that requires forms of consent, attribution, and redistribution. SASL signs represent local context and embed Deaf community identities.

Licensing, in this view, becomes an instrument for articulating those requirements and for ensuring that technological innovation does not proceed at the expense of cultural and linguistic integrity. By clearly specifying the terms under which SASL datasets may be used, conditions can be created under which Deaf individuals and organisations can retain a degree of agency over the systems being developed in their name.

6.3 Understanding the License

The decision to recommend the CC BY-NC-SA framework aligns with international best practices in managing culturally sensitive data, particularly in contexts involving Indigenous and minority languages. Several scholars have highlighted the importance of license design in mitigating extractive research practices and ensuring that digital resources reflect ethical relationships of collaboration and consent (Trejo *et al.,* 2021; Breaux & Alspaugh, 2011).

The CC BY-NC-SA licence establishes a publicly accessible governance structure that regulates the use, adaptation, and redistribution of resources under a set of clearly defined ethical conditions. Specifically, it requires users to (1) provide attribution to the original contributors, (2) refrain from using the material for commercial purposes without prior authorisation, and (3) release any derivative works under the same licensing terms. Each clause has distinct obligations that together constitute a mechanism for ensuring that the participation and recognition within the technological development landscape are fair and representative (Soylu & Şahin, 2024; Okolo, 2023). On the one hand, technologies for the public good should serve the public, maintain credit where it is due, and be safe and fit for purpose. Again, the objective is not to exploit the information, and it is to truly serve the community as well as advance technology in this context.

The attribution requirement affirms the intellectual contributions of Deaf researchers, community participants, and linguistic experts involved in developing SASL datasets and tools. In research domains where minority language contributors have often been structurally rendered invisible, formal attribution functions as a corrective mechanism that recognises marginalised knowledge production and situates it within broader epistemic systems (Datta, 2018). Recognition is not limited to symbolic value; it plays a substantive role in building reputational capital and asserting ownership over linguistic and cultural assets. Researchers and collaborators within various domains are required to show their research impact, and acknowledgement is one of these mechanisms.

The non-commercial clause delineates a boundary between uses motivated by public interest and those driven by private economic gain. It functions to prevent the extraction of community-derived resources by commercial actors who may profit from them without appropriate forms of consultation, compensation, or reinvestment. As documented in various studies of low-resource language contexts, the absence of such safeguards has led to the commodification of linguistic data in ways that exclude the originating communities from downstream benefits (Mlambo & Matfunjwa, 2024; Danaher *et al.,* 2013). The clause obliges commercial users to negotiate separate terms, potentially including financial compensation, ethical review processes, or community benefit-sharing agreements, thus introducing a level of procedural fairness.

The share-alike provision extends the ethical logic of the licence by mandating that any modifications, translations, or augmentations of SASL resources be re-released under identical conditions. This ensures that iterative developments remain within an open-access framework and are not subject to re-closure or commercial enclosure in later versions. It also contributes to the formation of a cumulative knowledge commons that prioritises mutual accountability and long-term accessibility (Breaux & Alspaugh, 2011).

The CC BY-NC-SA framework is also designed to accommodate evolving socio-technical and legal contexts. As standards for responsible AI, community data governance, and participatory research continue to develop globally, the licensing model can be adapted through consultative mechanisms. This includes the potential for revision of commercial licensing procedures, clarification of breach consequences, and the development of conflict resolution pathways. Such flexibility reflects a commitment to licensing not as a fixed constraint, but as an evolving tool of governance that must remain responsive to context (Verhulst *et al.,* 2025).

Positioning SASL human language technology development under the CC BY-NC-SA licence aligns with open science, data justice, and ethical ML (Coleman, 2023; Breaux & Alspaugh, 2011). Ultimately, the proposed licensing approach does not seek to limit the expansion of SASL technologies but to ensure that such expansion remains socially legitimate and institutionally accountable. It provides a normative structure through which technological progress may proceed in alignment with the values, aspirations, and collective agency of the various Deaf communities in South Africa.

6.4 A Future-Based Case Study

To outline how CC BY-NC-SA can be applied, let us outline a hypothetical case for exploring how the CC BY-NC-SA licensing frameworks might function in practice. Let us assume that in the coming years, a consortium of South African academic institutions will likely undertake a collaborative effort to create a large-scale, annotated SASL dataset to be used as AI training data. This initiative will aim to support research in human language technology, linguistic theory, human-computer interaction, and computer vision, while ensuring that Deaf communities retain a meaningful role in data governance. To guide the ethical management of this resource, suppose the project team will implement a CC BY-NC-SA licence.

The terms of this licence will be applied to the entire corpus, including videos, annotations, and metadata files. Its purpose will be to regulate the circulation of the dataset in a way that supports academic and non-profit use, while preventing the unregulated commercialisation of SASL linguistic data. First, all the contributors, including the Deaf community members, linguists, and data annotators, will be properly credited in the dataset documentation. This means that every output produced (credit and non-credit bearing) will include all these collaborators. It must be decided upon by the members involved how the accreditation will take place. Citation templates will be provided alongside each download, and a public contributor registry will be maintained to acknowledge participation across roles and institutions (Datta, 2018).

Second, there will be fewer restrictions on the dataset used in non-commercial domains such as education, research, and public service than in commercial, specifically around financing. Any for-profit organisation interested in integrating the dataset into proprietary platforms, such as avatar-based translation systems or commercial assistive apps, will be required to enter into a separate licensing agreement and pay for access and use of this data. These agreements will likely include provisions for financial compensation, the hiring of Deaf consultants, and commitments to equitable redistribution of benefits. This separation of use contexts will make explicit the ethical differences between public interest research and commercial innovation (Mlambo & Matfunjwa, 2024; Soylu & Şahin, 2024).

Third, derivative datasets, trained models, or adaptations are released under the same licence. This means that any spin-off from the primary data will also form part of the license. This will prevent the enclosure of community-generated resources into closed-source tools and maintain continuity within an open-access development ecosystem. Often, when intellectual property is concerned, even a variation of the original patent might constitute it to be a novel contribution. Under this type of licensing agreement, all secondary sources of information and variations that arise from the primary data still fall under the same original licence agreement. As other research groups and institutions adapt the dataset, the share-alike clause will preserve the collective value of enhancements, making them available to new users on equitable terms (Breaux & Alspaugh, 2011).

To oversee these licensing provisions, the project team will establish a community ethics review panel composed of scholars and representatives of all communities, especially Deaf scholars, legal experts, and digital rights advocates. This body will evaluate commercial requests, mediate disputes, and propose licensing amendments as technological and legal contexts evolve. The community ethics review pane will act not only as an oversight mechanism but as a space for deliberating the evolving norms of ethical data sharing in SASL technologies. This review panel may be national and can be part of the team that drives an overarching Deaf-centric research agenda. That is, an agenda that focuses on the future and the focus of research within these domains, especially human language technology.

As a result of these governance mechanisms, the SASL dataset will become a shared national South African asset (Mokofe, 2023). Assets need to be protected, governed, and maintained. It will be integrated into teaching materials, used in research, and adapted by local non-profits for accessibility initiatives. Importantly, it will remain protected from unilateral commercial capture, establishing a model of community-led data stewardship that resists extractive innovation logics.

While academic institutions may prioritise openness, collaboration, and public interest when curating SASL datasets, entrepreneurs engaging with the same resources operate within a different set of incentives. These actors are typically driven by innovation and commercial viability, often seeking to develop tools and platforms that can be monetised, such as real-time translation applications, accessibility services, or sign language-enabled virtual assistants. In this context, the application of the CC BY-NC-SA licence becomes essential in preventing the appropriation of community-generated linguistic data without fair compensation or ethical oversight.

Consider if a South African technology entrepreneur identifies an opportunity to build a SASL-to-text mobile application using an openly available dataset created by a consortium and licensed under CC BY-NC-SA. Recognising the market demand for inclusive communication tools, particularly in the educational and public service sectors, the entrepreneur begins developing a proprietary interface, improving model performance, and integrating voice-to-sign components aimed at commercial clients.

Under the terms of the licence, the entrepreneur may access the dataset and conduct preliminary experimentation; however, any application of the data for profit-oriented purposes, including the distribution of the app through paid services or freemium platforms, will trigger the non-commercial clause. This clause prohibits the use of the dataset in commercial products unless a separate commercial licence is negotiated. The obligation to enter into such a licensing agreement ensures that the people who contributed to the creation of the dataset, many of whom are Deaf signers, community validators, and linguists, are not excluded from the value chain of a commercial product that depends on their linguistic labour (Mlambo & Matfunjwa, 2024; Soylu & Şahin, 2024).

Intellectual property will be difficult to determine from a monetisation perspective; therefore, the inherent value of the commercialisation should be determined on an ad-hoc basis. For example, not all technologies that are developed for the market will potentially generate large revenue, but if the technology requires the SASL public dataset, then a community ethics review panel should serve as an enabler for the innovation. This means the purpose of the community ethics review panel should be to mitigate exploitation, enable innovation, and drive an overarching SASL human language technology research agenda.

6.5 Community Ethics Review Panels

The following key steps outline a systematic approach for institutions, project leaders, research groups, and custodial bodies charged with managing SASL human language resources and an overarching research agenda for SASL human language technologies. This framework is designed to support the ethical implementation and enforcement of the CC BY-NC-SA licence across all phases of SASL human language technology development. All SASL datasets, models, publications, software, and derivative works must prominently display their licensing status. Attribution to the CC BY-NC-SA licence must be consistently embedded within metadata, documentation headers, README files, user interfaces, and public-facing dissemination materials. Custodial authorities should provide standardised attribution templates to ensure consistent and correct crediting of contributors.

Templates must include the names of creators, institutional affiliations, dataset titles, date of creation, and licence terms. Versions adapted for academic publications, software repositories, websites, and media platforms should be readily available to all users. Effective governance requires informed compliance. Awareness campaigns should be embedded in postgraduate curricula, researcher onboarding processes, developer toolkits, and policy engagement activities. Workshops, digital guides, and multilingual resources should be tailored for diverse audiences, including Deaf community members, researchers, and industry partners, and should clarify licensing obligations and ethical norms. Access to restricted or unpublished SASL resources must be formalised through data access agreements that explicitly reference the CC BY-NC-SA licence.

These agreements must require users to affirm understanding and acceptance of the licensing conditions. Where appropriate, additional clauses addressing privacy, cultural sensitivity, and data protection should supplement the licence. Custodial entities must establish systems for ongoing monitoring of how SASL resources are cited, modified, and distributed. This includes automated citation tracking, periodic audits of academic publications and commercial platforms, and the use of embedded licensing metadata for digital traceability. Monitoring ensures that deviations from licence conditions can be identified and addressed promptly.

Clear enforcement protocols are necessary to address licence violations. These should include formal warning and corrective notification procedures for minor breaches (e.g., missing attribution), legal intervention for significant violations (e.g., unauthorised commercial use), and publication of breach summaries in annual reports to support transparency and institutional accountability. A structured process should be established for evaluating requests for commercial use of SASL resources. Applicants must submit detailed proposals outlining the nature of commercial use, anticipated revenue models, ethical compliance strategies, and benefit-sharing mechanisms. A review panel composed of Deaf leaders, linguists, and technology experts should assess proposals using transparent, pre-established criteria. All approved agreements must be legally binding and enforceable under South African intellectual property and contract law. Licensing governance must remain responsive to technological developments and shifting community priorities. An annual review process should be instituted to evaluate the efficacy of current practices, incorporate feedback from stakeholders, and revise protocols accordingly. Updates may include amendments to enforcement guidelines, templates, licensing language, or monitoring procedures. SASL human language technology custodians should actively engage with international standards and data ethics communities. This includes participation in networks such as Creative Commons Global, the Open Knowledge Foundation, and AI ethics consortia. Alignment with global best practices enhances institutional capacity, strengthens ethical credibility, and facilitates knowledge exchange across linguistic and technological domains.

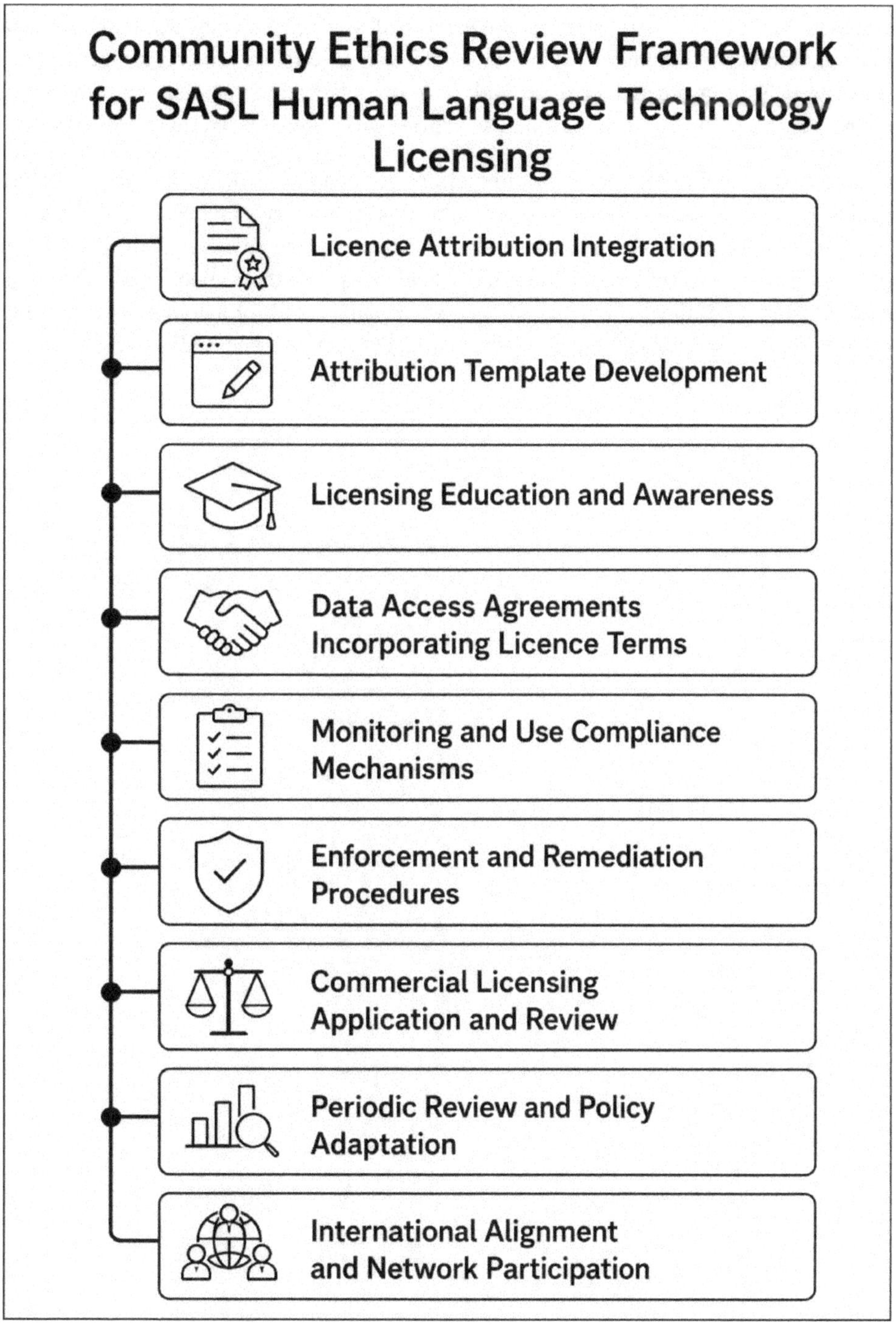

***Figure 6.1**: Framework for SASL human language technology licencing.*

The implementation of a structured licensing and governance framework is essential to ensure that SASL human language technologies are developed ethically, equitably, and with full recognition of community contributions. Effective governance requires clear attribution standards, education and awareness initiatives, formal data access agreements, monitoring systems, enforcement mechanisms, and structured processes for commercial licensing.

Periodic review and alignment with international standards further ensure that licensing remains responsive and globally informed. Collectively, these measures establish a proactive and rights-based approach to SASL human language technology development, grounded in accountability, transparency, and community leadership. We therefore would recommend the establishment of these proposed ethics review panels, and for a community buy-in to use the proposed licence agreement when SASL research is concerned.

CHAPTER 7

A Call to Action

Dr. Herkulaas Combrink

7.1 Skills Deficit in SASL Human Language Technology Development and the Need for Curriculum Development

The advancement of human language technology for South African Sign Language (SASL) is significantly constrained by a systemic shortage of interdisciplinary expertise. Across the research, development, and deployment continuum, there exists a pronounced gap in professionals proficient in Deaf studies, linguistic theory, artificial intelligence (AI), and software engineering. This fragmentation has hindered the integration of linguistic and computational knowledge, resulting in constrained project scope, underdeveloped technological outputs, and minimal academic engagement with SASL human language technology (Coy *et al.,* 2024; Joksimoski *et al.,* 2022). As argued within the book, the human language technology infodemic might be pervasive, but it can be stopped with scientific advancement, collaboration, and community participation.

Presently, South Africa lacks a formalised educational pathway designed to train individuals, both Deaf or hearing, at the confluence of SASL linguistics and computational technologies. Computer science and data science programmes remain structurally oriented toward hearing students, seldom incorporating accessible methodologies or academic programmes relevant to signed languages. Conversely, linguistics programmes that include SASL tend to emphasise theoretical frameworks over computational application, creating a bifurcation in training that undermines the development of well-rounded practitioners (Mashwama & Madubela, 2024; Ubido *et al.,* 2002). This structural disconnect limits the pool of professionals capable of contributing meaningfully to sign language technology development and perpetuates a scarcity of linguistically and ethically competent researchers.

To address this skills deficit, a dedicated interdisciplinary curriculum is urgently required, one that combines core principles of sign language linguistics, computational linguistics, human language technology, and Deaf cultural knowledge. Such a curriculum must be inclusive by design, integrating accessible teaching strategies, bilingual instruction, and adaptive resources to accommodate both Deaf and hearing students. Practical training components should extend beyond theoretical content to include data annotation, software development for sign languages, ethical data governance, and the evaluation of AI systems in multimodal, multilingual environments (McBride *et al.,* 2021; Mehler *et al.,* 2023).

Key curricular modules should encompass the phonological, morphological, and syntactic structures of SASL, sociolinguistic variation across Deaf communities, ethical research practices involving Deaf participants, foundational programming languages like Python, introductory and intermediate machine learning (ML) concepts, computer vision and motion capture techniques, annotation protocols specific to signed languages, and methods for generating synthetic datasets for under-resourced sign languages (Bragg *et al.,* 2021; Fenlon *et al.,* 2015). Importantly, such content must treat SASL not merely as a visual mode of communication but as a fully realised natural language with its own grammatical complexity and cultural significance.

Outcome-oriented curriculum design should align with the operational needs of the human language technology sector, enabling graduates to participate in SASL dataset development, AI model training, annotation, systems design, linguistic documentation, and accessibility evaluation. To ensure relevance and responsiveness, academic institutions must form strategic partnerships with Deaf-led organisations, research centres, and technology companies. These collaborations could manifest as internship opportunities, industry-aligned final-year projects, and guest lectures by professionals actively engaged in the design and deployment of human language technologies for sign languages (Reagan, 2020).

Furthermore, vertical integration with postgraduate study pathways should be established, allowing students to pursue advanced degrees in sign language human language technologies. Institutional support mechanisms, including targeted scholarships, mentorship structures, and academic accommodations, are essential for facilitating equitable access and supporting the emergence of Deaf scholars in this domain (Kohnke & Zaugg, 2025). Without concerted shifts in government resource allocations, these ideals might not be realised.

The creation of such a specialised curriculum is not secondary to the goals of digital inclusion or linguistic preservation,; it is central to ensuring the sustainable and ethical development of human language technologies for SASL. Without deliberate investment in training infrastructure, the long-term viability of SASL technologies will remain compromised, reinforcing existing disparities in technological access and inhibiting the realisation of AI's transformative potential for the Deaf community in South Africa.

7.2 Integrated Deaf Internships

The establishment of integrated internship programmes specifically designed for Deaf participants is essential for bridging the gap between academic training and professional engagement in the development of SASL human language technologies.

While curriculum development provides the foundational theoretical and technical knowledge, internships offer the applied, situated learning necessary to operationalise those skills in real-world settings (Turell, 2025; Marshall *et al.,* 2016). By embedding Deaf interns within live projects and interdisciplinary teams, these programmes create environments where experiential learning, mentorship, and technical collaboration are mutually reinforcing.

To be effective, such internships must be tailored to the specific demands of Deaf candidates operating within the interdisciplinary field of human language technology development. Placement models should avoid assigning Deaf interns to marginal or non-technical roles. Instead, they must be positioned as active contributors to research, data annotation, ML development, ethical review processes, and software deployment.

Involving Deaf interns in the full project lifecycle not only improves technical proficiency but also enhances epistemic inclusivity within project teams (Nihei, 2022). These roles also facilitate situated learning across disciplines, such as linguistics, computer science, and Deaf Studies, whilst reflecting the complexity of the human language technology innovation processes. Human language technologies are difficult to conceptualise and create. The presence of Deaf professionals or qualified CODAs (Children of Deaf Adults) as mentors can offer accessible guidance, model professional trajectories, and contribute to identity-affirming mentorship that supports intern efficacy.

In cases where internal Deaf mentors are unavailable, institutions must establish partnerships with external Deaf organisations or networks to facilitate hybrid or virtual mentorship support (Braun *et al.,* 2017). This ensures that all Deaf interns receive sustained support, irrespective of institutional capacity.

Ensuring accessibility within the workplace is non-negotiable for the success of integrated internships. Host institutions are ethically and legally obligated to implement inclusive practices, including the provision of SASL interpreters, captioning systems, visual communication tools, and workspaces designed in consultation with Deaf professionals. Furthermore, accessibility training must be provided to all hearing colleagues involved in hosting Deaf interns. This training should encompass Deaf cultural awareness, communication strategies, and institutional responsibility under disability inclusion frameworks (Vohra *et al.,* 2015).

Internships should also be explicitly aligned with longer-term career development objectives. Deaf interns must have opportunities to build technical portfolios, co-author publications, present at conferences, and engage with grant-writing or entrepreneurial training. This approach ensures that internships function not as isolated learning events, but as platforms for sustained career trajectories. Universities and research institutes must establish formal pathways from internships into postgraduate study, employment, or research assistantships, supported by mentorship and financial aid structures (Ellis-Robinson, 2021).

To operationalise integrated internships at scale, robust partnerships are required between universities, research organisations, technology companies, and Deaf advocacy bodies. A coordinated national strategy would allow for pooled resources, consistent standards, and broad access. Financial or institutional incentives, such as tax benefits, public recognition schemes, or prioritisation in government research funding, could further incentivise participation from private and public stakeholders (Barnes & Mercer, 1997).

Comprehensive monitoring and evaluation must be embedded within all internship programmes to ensure accountability and continuous improvement. Longitudinal tracking of career pathways is essential to determine whether internships effectively contribute to the development of Deaf leadership within the SASL human language technology field (Fontana & Mitra, 2023).

7.3 Onboarding Deaf Data Scientists

The successful advancement of SASL human language technology research demands not only the development of foundational skills and internship opportunities but also the establishment of intentional, structured, and accessible onboarding processes specifically tailored for Deaf data scientists. The current absence of onboarding programmes represents a missed opportunity to harness the unique linguistic and cultural knowledge that Deaf professionals bring to the field of AI and human language technology development. Effective onboarding of Deaf data scientists is not merely about technical orientation; it is about embedding them meaningfully into interdisciplinary research environments, ensuring their career progression, and empowering them to shape the direction of human language technology innovation.

Onboarding Deaf data scientists requires an approach that is fundamentally different from generic induction programmes designed for hearing professionals. The onboarding process must begin with an initial needs assessment to understand the preferred communication methods, learning styles, and support requirements of each Deaf data scientist. Such assessments should inform the design of personalised onboarding pathways, ensuring that training materials, mentorship models, and workplace technologies are adapted to facilitate full participation from the outset.

An effective onboarding programme should comprise several distinct phases, beginning with orientation to the institutional environment. Deaf data scientists must be introduced not only to organisational structures and policies but also to the specific projects, methodologies, and ethical frameworks governing human language technology research. This includes familiarisation with annotation conventions for SASL data, ML pipelines used in sign language technologies, best practices in bias mitigation, and accessibility standards for AI system outputs. Comprehensive documentation, presented in bilingual formats and supported by visual resources, should be made readily available to ensure clarity and ease of reference. Each Deaf data scientist should be paired with an experienced mentor, ideally someone with expertise in computational linguistics, AI, or Deaf Studies, who can provide both technical guidance and professional development support. Mentorship relationships should be structured, with regular check-ins, goal-setting exercises, and opportunities for collaborative work on meaningful projects. Where possible, peer mentoring networks among Deaf and hearing researchers should be encouraged to enable a sense of professional community and reduce isolation.

The onboarding phase must also address the specific technical competencies required for success in the human language technology domain. Tailored workshops should be provided covering advanced ML techniques relevant to sign language applications for video-based recognition, natural language processing pipelines for gloss-based translation, and synthetic data generation methods for augmentation of under-resourced datasets. Hands-on coding sessions, hackathons, and collaborative sprints can serve as powerful platforms for skill-building while simultaneously strengthening team cohesion. Accessibility considerations must be deeply embedded throughout the onboarding process. All meetings, training sessions, and collaborative activities should include SASL interpretation, real-time captioning, or other accessible communication supports. Project management and collaboration tools should be selected or adapted to ensure full usability by Deaf professionals, incorporating visual design principles and asynchronous communication options where possible. Staff and team members should receive ongoing sensitisation training to enhance communication fluency and cultural competency when working alongside Deaf colleagues.

Importantly, onboarding should not be a time-limited activity but rather the beginning of an ongoing process of support, reflection, and growth. Regular feedback loops should be instituted to allow Deaf data scientists to share their experiences of the onboarding process, identify gaps, and recommend improvements. Institutions must commit to continuously adapting and evolving their onboarding practices based on lived experience feedback, ensuring that future cohorts benefit from a progressively more inclusive and empowering environment.

Strategically onboarding Deaf data scientists is essential not only for achieving technical excellence in SASL human language technology research but for embedding principles of equity, representation, and linguistic justice at the heart of technological innovation. By investing in comprehensive, accessible, and empowering onboarding programmes, institutions can cultivate a new generation of Deaf leaders whose presence and perspectives will fundamentally enrich the trajectory of AI and human language technologies for the Deaf community and society at large.

7.4 Managing the Deaf Human Language Technology Infodemic

In an era where digital communication infrastructures shape public understanding, institutional agendas, and technological legitimacy, there is a critical need to systematically monitor and analyse social media platforms and public discourse to ensure that narratives surrounding Deaf human language technologies, particularly those involving SASL, do not become enmeshed in a new form of linguistic and technological infodemic (Cinelli *et al.,* 2020; Tangcharoensathien *et al.,* 2021). In the context of under-represented language communities and AI development, a parallel phenomenon may emerge wherein exaggerated claims, misinformed representations, and commercially motivated hype about Deaf communities circulate without critical scrutiny, resulting in distorted public perceptions, misaligned funding priorities, exclusion of Deaf epistemologies, and unethical appropriation of linguistic resources. As SASL gains legal and sociopolitical visibility within South Africa, and as ML, avatar development, and gesture recognition systems receive increased public and commercial attention, there is a growing potential for the weaponisation of discourse, whereby Deaf language technologies are framed not as community-led initiatives but as market-driven innovations detached from their social origins. Narratives that fail to accurately represent the linguistic, cultural, and ethical complexities of SASL can lead to decisions that privilege technical feasibility over justice, and reify colonial tropes of deficit, accessibility-as-charity, and passive data contribution (Verhulst *et al.,* 2025; Tomalin *et al.,* 2023).

7.5 Conclusion

The future of SASL in human language technology will be shaped by the choices and commitments made today. The technological landscape is evolving rapidly, and unless decisive action is taken to address long-standing gaps in skills development, structural inclusion, and research governance, the Deaf community risks being excluded from the very innovations that could support their linguistic and cultural flourishing. This chapter has put forward an urgent appeal for systemic transformation, a shift that centres Deaf knowledge, interdisciplinary collaboration, and ensures that SASL is not merely accommodated within the digital era but thrives as a driver of innovation and equity.

Building this future begins with reimagining education. South Africa must develop dedicated academic pathways that prepare both Deaf and hearing students to engage meaningfully with the complex intersection of linguistics, AI, and Deaf culture. These pathways must not be add-ons to existing programmes, but fully integrated curricula that reflect the unique competencies required for SASL human language technological development. Without such foundational structures, the sector will continue to struggle with fragmentation, exclusion, and underutilised talent.

Yet, education alone is not enough. To bridge the divide between academic learning and professional participation, structured Deaf internships must become a core feature of the SASL human language technology pipeline. These internships should offer more than exposure; they must provide real responsibility, robust mentorship, accessible environments, and long-term career opportunities. In such spaces, Deaf interns can grow into future leaders, shaping the direction of research and development from the inside. In parallel, the integration of Deaf data scientists into research and industry spaces requires a complete rethinking of traditional onboarding approaches. Institutions must move beyond symbolic inclusion and invest in strategies that actively develop and retain Deaf talent. This includes designing accessible, tailored pathways that recognise and cultivate the technical, cultural, and leadership contributions Deaf professionals bring to the table. Embedding Deaf expertise into the heart of innovation ecosystems is not just about inclusion; it is about shifting the balance of power and reconfiguring who gets to shape technological futures.

At a structural level, enduring change depends on institutionalising community governance. With the power to influence funding decisions, endorse research initiatives, and shape public policy, such a committee would safeguard the linguistic integrity of SASL and amplify Deaf leadership in national and global technology debates.

We are at a critical juncture in the convergence of AI, linguistics, and Deaf Studies. The possibilities are vast, but so too are the risks. Without conscious, inclusive planning, these technologies may reproduce the very exclusions they promise to dismantle. But with foresight, care, and commitment, SASL can become a space of empowerment, where innovation advances not only technical goals, but social justice, linguistic diversity, and cultural recognition. The responsibility does not rest solely with computer scientists or linguists. This is a collective project, one that calls on educators, policymakers, researchers, developers, funders, and advocates alike. It requires that we ask hard questions about who sets research agendas, whose knowledge counts, and what values guide our innovations. It asks us to imagine and then build a research culture around SASL human language technologies.

This vision will take time. It will require sustained investment, trust-building, and commitment to partnership. South Africa now stands at the threshold of a global opportunity. By leading the way in how signed languages and Deaf communities are meaningfully included in the digital age, the country can set a precedent that resonates far beyond its borders. The tools are available. The expertise exists. The urgency is real. *The time to act is now!*

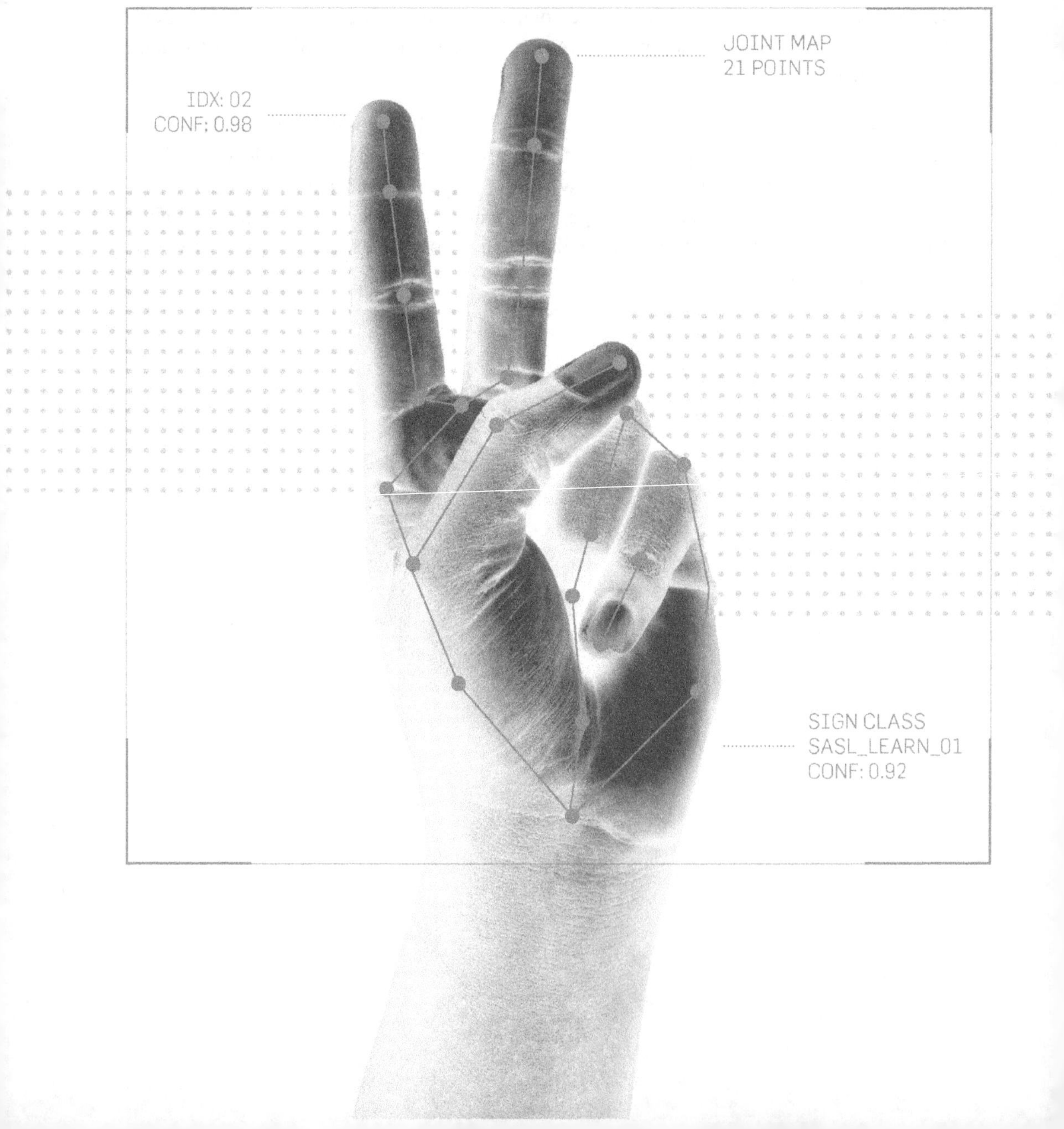
JOINT MAP
21 POINTS
IDX: 02
CONF: 0.98
SIGN CLASS
SASL_LEARN_01
CONF: 0.92

EPILOGUE

As the frontiers of technology continue to expand, the responsibility to ensure justice, inclusion, and ethical stewardship becomes not merely an academic concern but a moral imperative. South African Sign Language (SASL) is not simply a linguistic system; it is a vessel of identity, memory, and resistance. Its integration into the fabric of twenty-first-century innovation must be pursued not as an act of charity, but as a matter of equity and cultural survival.

The future will not be shaped solely by algorithms, datasets, or institutions, but by the people who dare to ask: Whose voices are missing, and what futures are possible when they are heard?

This book closes, but the real work begins.

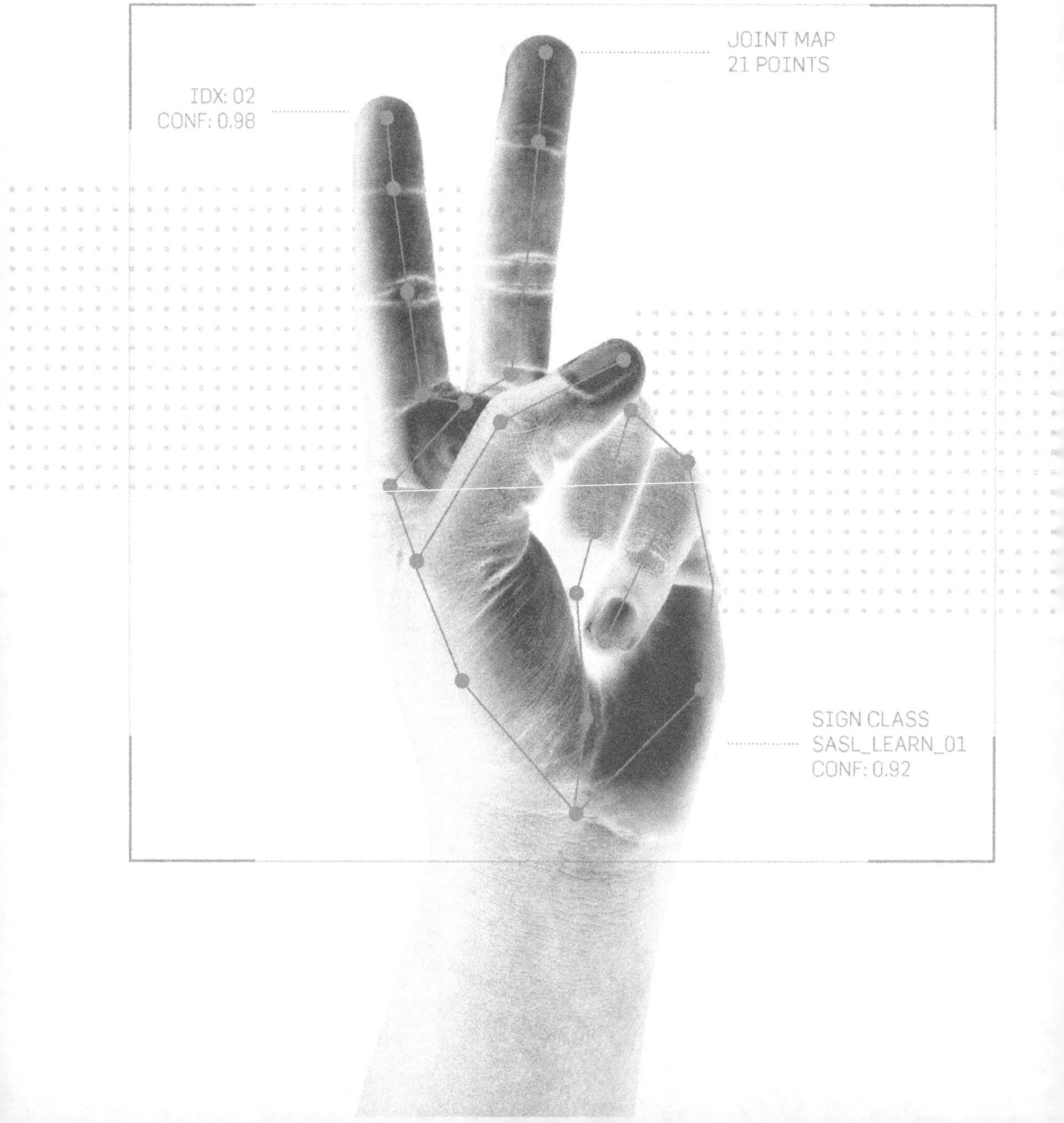
JOINT MAP
21 POINTS
IDX: 02
CONF: 0.98
SIGN CLASS
SASL_LEARN_01
CONF: 0.92

CLOSING DEDICATION

For the South African Deaf community.

For the scientists advancing technology.

For the storytellers, the educators, the researchers, the activists, the quiet innovators, and the bold disruptors.

For those who have preserved SASL through silence and resistance.

For those building futures where Deaf knowledge leads.

This work is yours.

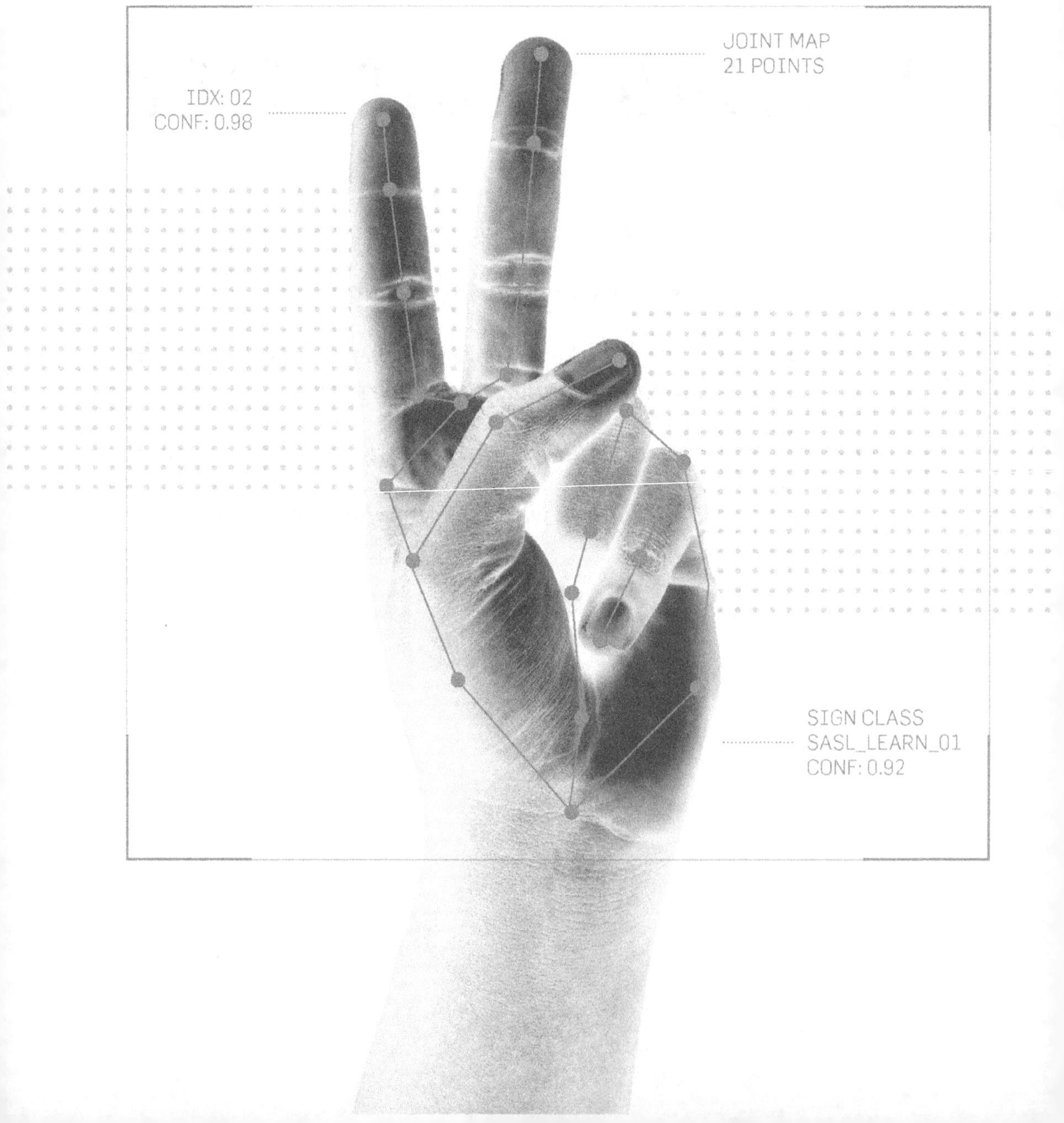
JOINT MAP
21 POINTS
IDX: 02
CONF: 0.98
SIGN CLASS
SASL_LEARN_01
CONF: 0.92

REFERENCES

1. James, G., Witten, D., Hastie, T. and Tibshirani, R., 2013. *An introduction to statistical learning: with applications in R*. New York: Springer.

2. LeCun, Y., Bengio, Y. and Hinton, G., 2015. Deep learning. *Nature*, *521*(7553), pp.436–444. Available at: https://doi.org/10.1038/nature14539.

3. Choi, R.Y., Coyner, A.S., Kalpathy-Cramer, J., Chiang, M.F. and Campbell, J.P., 2020. Introduction to machine learning, neural networks, and deep learning. *Translational Vision Science & Technology*, 9(2), p.14. Available at: https://doi.org/10.1167/tvst.9.2.14.

4. Hinton, G.E., and Salakhutdinov, R.R., 2006. Reducing the dimensionality of data with neural networks. *Science*, *313*(5786), pp.504–507. https://doi.org/10.1126/science.1127647.

5. Ghosh, S., Das, N., Das, I. and Maulik, U., 2019. Understanding deep learning techniques for image segmentation. *arXiv preprint*. http://arxiv.org/abs/1907.06119.

6. Zhang, Q. and Zhu, S.-C., 2018. Visual interpretability for deep learning: a survey. *arXiv preprint*. http://arxiv.org/abs/1802.00614.

7. Abiteboul, S., 1997. Querying semi-structured data. In: *Proceedings of the Sixth International Conference on Database Theory (ICDT)*. Greece: Springer.

8. Adebesin, F., Smuts, H., Mawela, T., Maramba, G. and Hattingh, M., 2023. The role of social media in health misinformation and disinformation during the COVID-19 pandemic: bibliometric analysis. *JMIR Infodemiology*, *3*(1), p.e48620.

9. Takyi, K., Gyening, R.M.O.M., Gueuwou, S.M., Nyarko, M.S., Adade, R., Borkor, R.N., Boadu-Acheampong, S.I., and Tabari, L., 2025. AfriSign: African sign languages machine translation. *Discover Artificial Intelligence*, *5*(1), p.6.

10. Agrawal, D., Buhmann, J., Borer, D., Sumner, R.W. and Guay, M., 2024. SKEL-Betweener: a neural motion rig for interactive motion authoring. *ACM Transactions on Graphics (TOG)*, *43*(6), pp.1–11.

11. Akach, P.A.O., 2010. *Application of South African Sign Language (SASL) in a bilingual-bicultural approach in education of the Deaf.* (PhD thesis, University of the Free State).

12. Alam, I., Hameed, A. and Ziar, R.A., 2024. Exploring Sign Language detection on smartphones: a systematic review of machine and deep learning approaches. *Advances in Human-Computer Interaction*, *2024*(1), p.1487500.

13. Alloghani, M., Al-Jumeily, D., Mustafina, J., Hussain, A. and Aljaaf, A.J., 2020. A systematic review on supervised and unsupervised machine learning algorithms for data science. In: *supervised and unsupervised learning for data science*, pp.3–21.

14. Alonso, M.A., Gómez-Rodríguez, C. and Vilares, J., 2021. On the use of parsing for named entity recognition. *Applied Sciences*, *11*(3), p.1090.

15. Amin, M., Hefny, H. and Ammar, M., 2021. Sign language gloss translation using deep learning models. *International Journal of Advanced Computer Science and Applications, 12*(11).

16. Andrade, V.D. and Baloyi, B., 2011. "Some of the things I understand but not all of it". A group of deaf adolescents' sources of knowledge and concerns regarding the adequacy of their level of knowledge about HIV/AIDS. *Vulnerable Children and Youth Studies, 6*(3), pp.255–262.

17. Arun Prasath, G. and Annapurani, K., 2023. Prediction of sign language recognition based on multi-layered CNN. *Multimedia Tools and Applications, 82*(19), pp.29649–29669.

18. Aslam, U., Batool, E., Ahsan, S.N. and Sultan, A., 2017. Hybrid network intrusion detection system using machine learning classification and rule-based learning system. *International Journal of Grid and Distributed Computing, 10*(2), pp.51–62.

19. Barcelona, V., Scharp, D., Idnay, B.R., Moen, H., Cato, K. and Topaz, M., 2024. Identifying stigmatizing language in clinical documentation: a scoping review of emerging literature. *PLOS ONE, 19*(6), p.e0303653.

20. Danaher, M., Cook, J., Danaher, G., Coombes, P. and Danaher, P.A., 2013. Researching ethically and responsibly with marginalized communities. *Researching education with marginalized communities*, pp.134-151.

21. Bartlett, B. and Bartlett, J., 2016. *Practical recording techniques: the step-by-step approach to professional audio recording*. 6th ed. London: Routledge.

22. Bauman, H.D.L. and Murray, J.J., 2013. Deaf studies in the 21st century:'Deaf-gain'and the future of human diversity. *The Disability Studies Reader, 4*, pp.246-262.

23. Bengio, Y., Courville, A. and Vincent, P., 2013. Representation learning: a review and new perspectives. *IEEE Transactions on Pattern Analysis and Machine Intelligence, 35*(8), pp.1798–1828.

24. Benjamin, R., 2022. *Viral justice: how we grow the world we want.* Princeton, NJ: Princeton University Press.

25. Bentéjac, C., Csörgő, A. and Martínez-Muñoz, G., 2021. A comparative analysis of gradient boosting algorithms. *Artificial Intelligence Review, 54*(3), pp.1937–1967. Available at: https://doi.org/10.1007/s10462-020-09896-5.

26. Berke, L., Kafle, S. and Huenerfauth, M., 2018. Methods for evaluation of imperfect captioning tools by deaf or hard-of-hearing users at different reading literacy levels. In: *Proceedings of the 2018 CHI Conference on Human Factors in Computing Systems*, pp.1–12.

27. Bernard, S., Heutte, L. and Adam, S., 2009. On the selection of decision trees in random forests. In: *2009 International Joint Conference on Neural Networks (IJCNN)*, Atlanta, GA, USA: IEEE, pp.302–307. Available at: https://doi.org/10.1109/IJCNN.2009.5178693.

28. Bianchini, C.S., 2021. How to improve metalinguistic awareness by writing a language without writing: Sign Languages and SignWriting. *Grapholinguistics and Its Applications, 5*(2), pp.1039–1065.

29. Bigi, B., 2011. A multilingual text normalization approach. In: *Language and Technology Conference*. Cham: Springer International Publishing, pp.515–526.

30. Bird, S., 2020. Decolonising speech and language technology. In: *Proceedings of the 28th International Conference on Computational Linguistics*, pp.3504–3519.

31. Blake, E., Tucker, W. and Glaser, M., 2014. Towards communication and information access for Deaf people. *South African Computer Journal, 54*(si-2), pp.10–19.

32. Bogatinovski, J., Todorovski, L., Džeroski, S. and Kocev, D., 2021. Comprehensive comparative study of multi-label classification methods. *arXiv preprint arXiv:2102.07113*: https://doi.org/10.1016/j.eswa.2022.117215.

33. Efthimiou, E., Fotinea, S.E., Hanke, T., Glauert, J., Bowden, R., Braffort, A., Collet, C., Maragos, P. and Lefebvre-Albaret, F., 2012. Sign Language technologies and resources of the Dicta-Sign project. In: *5th Workshop on the Representation and Processing of Sign Languages: Interactions between Corpus and Lexicon. Satellite Workshop to the Eighth International Conference on Language Resources and Evaluation (LREC-2012).*

34. Brentari, D., 2011. *Sign languages*. Cambridge: Cambridge University Press.

35. Brown, J.M., Campbell, J.P., Beers, A., et al., 2018. Automated diagnosis of plus disease in retinopathy of prematurity using deep convolutional neural networks. *JAMA Ophthalmology*, 136(7), pp.803–810. Available at: https://doi.org/10.1001/jamaophthalmol.2018.1934.

36. Brown, S.W., 1995. Time, change, and motion: the effects of stimulus movement on temporal perception. *Perception & Psychophysics*, *57*, pp.105–116.

37. Joksimoski, B., Zdravevski, E., Lameski, P., Pires, I.M., Melero, F.J., Martinez, T.P., Garcia, N.M., Mihajlov, M., Chorbev, I. and Trajkovik, V., 2022. Technological solutions for sign language recognition: a scoping review of research trends, challenges, and opportunities. *IEEE Access*, *10*, pp.40979-40998.

38. Buttar, A.M., Ahmad, U., Gumaei, A.H., Assiri, A., Akbar, M.A. and Alkhamees, B.F., 2023. Deep learning in sign language recognition: a hybrid approach for the recognition of static and dynamic signs. *Mathematics*, *11*(17), p.3729.

39. Camgoz, N.C., Hadfield, S., Koller, O., Ney, H. and Bowden, R., 2018. Neural sign language translation. In: *Proceedings of the IEEE conference on computer vision and pattern recognition* (pp. 7784-7793).

40. Camgoz, N.C., Hadfield, S., Koller, O., Ney, H. and Bowden, R., 2017. Subunets: end-to-end hand shape and continuous sign language recognition. In: *Proceedings of the IEEE international conference on computer vision* (pp. 3056-3065).

41. Carne, C., Oostendorp, M. and Baker, A., 2024. Ideological framing of sign languages and their users in the South African press. *Multilingua*, *43*(4), pp.525–552.

42. Center for Sutton Movement Writing, n.d. SignPuddle 2.0: Home Page. [online] Available at: http://www.signbank.org/signpuddle/index3.html [Accessed 16 May 2025].

43. Okolo, C.T., 2023. Addressing global inequity in AI development. In: *Handbook of critical studies of artificial intelligence* (pp. 378-389). Edward Elgar Publishing.

44. Chaurasia, V. and Pal, S., 2020. Machine learning algorithms using binary classification and multi- model ensemble techniques for skin diseases prediction. *International Journal of Biomedical Engineering and Technology, 34*(1), p.57. https://doi.org/10.1504/IJBET.2020.110361.

45. Chelliah, S.L. and De Reuse, W.J., 2010. *Handbook of descriptive linguistic fieldwork.* Springer Science & Business Media.

46. Chen, X., Lee, W. and Lin, F., 2022. Infodemic, institutional trust, and COVID-19 vaccine hesitancy: a cross-national survey. *International Journal of Environmental Research and Public Health, 19*(13), p.8033.

47. Ubido, J., Huntington, J. and Warburton, D., 2002. Inequalities in access to healthcare faced by women who are deaf. *Health & Social Care in the Community, 10*(4), pp.247-253.

48. Chiou, H., Voegeli, C., Wilhelm, E., Kolis, J., Brookmeyer, K. and Prybylski, D., 2022. The future of infodemic surveillance as public health surveillance. *Emerging Infectious Diseases, 28*(Suppl 1), p.S121.

49. Chowdhury, N., Khalid, A. and Turin, T.C., 2023. Understanding misinformation infodemic during public health emergencies due to large-scale disease outbreaks: a rapid review. Journal of Public Health, *31*(4), pp.553–573.

50. Al-Qurishi, M., Khalid, T. and Souissi, R., 2021. Deep learning for sign language recognition: current techniques, benchmarks, and open issues. *IEEE Access, 9*, pp.126917-126951.

51. Cinelli, M., Quattrociocchi, W., Galeazzi, A., Valensise, C.M., Brugnoli, E., Schmidt, A.L., Zola, P., Zollo, F. and Scala, A., 2020. The COVID-19 social media infodemic. *Scientific Reports, 10*(1), p.16598.

52. Breaux, T.D. and Alspaugh, T.A., 2011, August. Governance and accountability in the new data ecology. In: *2011 Fourth International Workshop on Requirements Engineering and Law* (pp. 5-14). IEEE.

53. Combrink, H., Loth, C.-R., Sibanda, P., Siyavoshi, S., Nkuna, N., Coetzee, N., et al., 2025. Reports for advancing South African Sign Language for 4IR technological development using place names. University of the Free State. https://doi.org/10.38140/ufs.28847498.v3.

54. Cooper, L., Fuzesi, P., Jacob, S.A., Kamalakannan, S., Lennon, M., Macaden, L., et al., 2023. Assistive technologies and strategies to support the medication management of individuals with hearing and/or visual impairment: a scoping review. *Disability and Health Journal, 16*(4), p.101500.

55. Ebling, S., Konrad, R., Braem, P.B. and Langer, G., 2015. Factors to consider when making lexical comparisons of sign languages: notes from an ongoing comparison of German Sign Language and Swiss German Sign Language. *Sign Language Studies, 16*(1), pp.30-56.

56. Cormier, K., Schembri, A., Vinson, D. and Orfanidou, E., 2012. First language acquisition differs from second language acquisition in prelingually deaf signers: evidence from syntactic and semantic processing. *Applied Psycholinguistics, 34*(5), pp.1045–1072.

57. Coy, A., 2022. Barriers to technology-enabled education for the Deaf in the Caribbean. In: *Equitable education for marginalized youth in Latin America and the Caribbean*, pp.155–185. London: Routledge.

58. Fenlon, J., Schembri, A., Johnston, T. and Cormier, K., 2015. Documentary and corpus approaches to sign language research. In: *Research methods in sign language studies: a practical guide*, pp.156-172.

59. Crasborn, O. and Sloetjes, H., 2008. Enhanced ELAN functionality for sign language corpora. In: *6th International Conference on Language Resources and Evaluation (LREC 2008)/3rd Workshop on the Representation and Processing of Sign Languages: Construction and Exploitation of Sign Language Corpora,* pp. 39-43.

60. Crystal, D., 2011. *A dictionary of linguistics and phonetics*. John Wiley & Sons.

61. Luo, J., 2022. Data-driven innovation: what is it?. *IEEE Transactions on Engineering Management*, *70*(2), pp.784-790.

62. de Beurs, Z.L., Islam, N., Gopalan, G. and Vrtilek, S.D., 2022. A comparative study of machine-learning methods for X-ray binary classification. *The Astrophysical Journal*, *933*(1), p.116.

63. de Beuzeville, L., Johnston, T. and Schembri, A., 2009. The use of space with indicating verbs in Auslan: a corpus-based approach. *Sign Language and Linguistics*, *12*(1), pp.53–82.

64. De Coster, M. and Dambre, J., 2022. Leveraging frozen pretrained written language models for neural sign language translation. *Information*, *13*(5), p.220.

65. Boyles, J. and Talbot, N., 2017. *Working with interpreters in psychological therapy: the right to be understood.* Routledge.

66. De Meulder, M., 2016. *The power of language policy: the legal recognition of sign languages and the aspirations of deaf communities* (No. 301). University of Jyväskylä.

67. Batterbury, S.C., 2012. Language justice for sign language peoples: the UN Convention on the Rights of Persons with Disabilities. *Language Policy*, *11*, pp.253-272.

68. Deng, L. and Yu, D., 2014. Deep learning: methods and applications. *Foundations and Trends in Signal Processing*, *7*(3–4), pp.197–387.

69. Desselle, D.D. and Proctor, T.K., 2000. Advocating for the elderly hard-of-hearing population: the deaf people we ignore. *Social Work*, *45*(3), pp.277-281.

70. Do Nascimento, I.J.B., Pizarro, A.B., Almeida, J.M., Azzopardi-Muscat, N., Gonçalves, M.A., Björklund, M. and Novillo-Ortiz, D., 2022. Infodemics and health misinformation: a systematic review of reviews. *Bulletin of the World Health Organization*, *100*(9), p.544.

71. Doshi-Velez, F. and Kim, B., 2017. Towards a rigorous science of interpretable machine learning. *arXiv preprint* arXiv:1702.08608.

72. Dreksler, B., Rędzińska, K., Rędziński, P. and Nalbandian, S., 2025. The diffusion of digital technologies in landscape planning - a scoping literature review. *Land Use Policy*, *154*, p.107549.

73. Elmasri, R. and Navathe, S.B., 2015. *Fundamentals of database systems*. 7th ed. London: Pearson.

74. Emmorey, K., 2001. *Language, cognition, and the brain: insights from sign language research.* Psychology Press.

75. Emmorey, K., Tversky, B. and Taylor, H.A., 2000. Using space to describe space: perspective in speech, sign, and gesture. *Spatial Cognition and Computation*, *2*, pp.157-180.

76. Encyclopædia Britannica, 2024. Latin alphabet. https://www.britannica.com/topic/Latin-alphabet.

77. Eysenbach, G., 2002. Infodemiology: the epidemiology of (mis)information. *The American Journal of Medicine*, *113*(9), pp.763–765.

78. Foggitt, I., 2000. SignWriting in South Africa. [online] SignWriting.org. Available at: https://www.signwriting.org/africa/africa001.html [Accessed 5 April 2025].

79. Foody, G.M. and Mathur, A., 2004. A relative evaluation of multiclass image classification by support vector machines. IEEE Transactions on Geoscience and Remote Sensing, *42*(6), pp.1335–1343.

80. Freitas, D., 2010. Accessibility and design for all solutions through speech technology. In: *Speech technology: theory and applications*, pp.271–299.

81. Fricker, E., 2006. Second-hand knowledge. *Philosophy and Phenomenological Research*, *73*(3), pp.592–618.

82. Friedman, J., Hastie, T. and Tibshirani, R., 2000. Additive logistic regression: a statistical view of boosting (with discussion and a rejoinder by the authors). *The Annals of Statistics*, *28*(2), pp.337-407.

83. Gandomi, A. and Haider, M., 2015. Beyond the hype: big data concepts, methods, and analytics. *International Journal of Information Management*, *35*(2), pp.137–144.

84. Genetti, C. and Adelman, A.S., 2019. *How languages work: an introduction to language and linguistics*. 2nd ed. Cambridge: Cambridge University Press.

85. Li, J. and Chignell, M., 2022. FMEA-AI: AI fairness impact assessment using failure mode and effects analysis. *AI and Ethics*, *2*(4), pp.837-850.

86. Baca, M. ed., 2016. *Introduction to metadata*. Getty Publications.

87. Global Partnership on AI (GPAI), 2022. Data justice: A primer on data and social justice. [online] https://gpai.ai/projects/data-governance/primer-on-data-and-social-justice.pdf.

88. Goyal, L. and Goyal, V., 2016. Text to Sign Language translation system: a review of literature. *International Journal of Synthetic Emotions (IJSE)*, *7*(2), pp.62–77.

89. Gramkow, F., 2023. The influence of age of acquisition and frequency of used words on a visual word recognition task. (Master's thesis, Insert university name).

90. Graves, A., 2013. Speech recognition with deep recurrent neural networks. In: *IEEE International Conference on Acoustics, Speech and Signal Processing (ICASSP)*, pp.6645–6649.

91. Gurkhe, D., Pal, N. and Bhatia, R., 2014. Effective sentiment analysis of social media datasets using Naive Bayesian classification. *International Journal of Computer Applications*, *99*(13), pp.1–4.

92. Verhulst, S., Zahuranec, A.J., Zable, A. and Addo, P., 2025. Reimagining data governance for AI: Operationalizing a social license for data reuse. Available at SSRN 5255677.

93. Gutierrez, A.K., 2017. Globalization and glocalization. In: *The Routledge Companion to International Children's Literature*, pp.11–21. London: Routledge.

94. Hanke, T., 2004. HamNoSys—Representing Sign Language data in language resources and language processing contexts. In: *LREC Workshop on Representation and Processing of Sign Languages.*

95. Hanke, T. and Storz, J., 2008. iLex—A database tool for integrating Sign Language corpus linguistics and Sign Language lexicography. In: *Proceedings of LREC 2008.*

96. Haricharan, H.J., Heap, M., Hacking, D. and Lau, Y.K., 2017. Health promotion via SMS improves hypertension knowledge for Deaf South Africans. *BMC Public Health, 17*, pp.1–17.

97. Hassan, A. and Mahmood, A., 2018. Convolutional recurrent deep learning model for sentence classification. *IEEE Access*, *6*, pp.13949–13957.

98. Hastie, T., Tibshirani, R., Friedman, J., Hastie, T., Tibshirani, R. and Friedman, J., 2009. Overview of supervised learning. *The elements of statistical learning: data mining, inference, and prediction*, pp.9-41.

99. Kahlon, N.K. and Singh, W., 2023. Machine translation from text to sign language: a systematic review. *Universal Access in the Information Society*, *22*(1), pp.1-35.

100. Heijungs, R., Guinée, J., Kleijn, R. and Rovers, V., 2007. Bias in normalization: causes, consequences, detection and remedies. *The International Journal of Life Cycle Assessment*, *12*, pp.211–216.

101. Nihei, M., 2022. Epistemic injustice as a philosophical conception for considering fairness and diversity in human-centered AI principles. *Interdisciplinary Information Sciences*, *28*(1), pp.35-43.

102. Klein, L. and D'Ignazio, C., 2024, June. Data feminism for AI. In: *Proceedings of the 2024 ACM Conference on Fairness, Accountability, and Transparency* (pp. 100-112).

103. Hummel, P., Braun, M., Tretter, M. and Dabrock, P., 2021. Data sovereignty: a review. *Big Data & Society*, *8*(1), p.2053951720982012.

104. Hodosh, M., Young, P. and Hockenmaier, J., 2013. Framing image description as a ranking task: data, models and evaluation metrics. *Journal of Artificial Intelligence Research*, *47*, pp.853–899.

105. Holcomb, L., Hall, W.C., Gardiner-Walsh, S.J. and Scott, J., 2025. Challenging the "norm": a critical look at Deaf-hearing comparison studies in research. *Journal of Deaf Studies and Deaf Education*, *30*(1), pp.2–16.

106. Holness, W., 2016. The development and use of Sign Language in South African schools: the denial of inclusive education. *African Disability Rights Yearbook*, *4*, p.141.

107. Huang, Y., Huang, J., Wu, X. and Jia, Y., 2022. Dynamic Sign Language recognition based on CBAM with autoencoder time series neural network. *Mobile Information Systems, 2022*(1), p.3247781.

108. Humphrey, A., Adams, J. and Hoetzlein, R., 2022. Developing techniques for rigging and motion capture to simplify 3D animation. *Aquila: The FGCU Student Undergraduate Research Journal*, pp.36–45.

109. Shand, R. and Bowden, A.B., 2022. Empirical support for establishing common assumptions in cost research in education. *Journal of Research on Educational Effectiveness, 15*(1), pp.103-129.

110. Iancu, B., et al., 2019. Multi-label classification for automatic tag prediction in the context of programming challenges. *arXiv preprint* arXiv:1911.12224.

111. Jachova, Z., Kovacheva, O. and Karovska, A., 2008. Differences between American Sign Language (ASL) and British Sign Language (BSL). *Journal of Special Education and Rehabilitation, 9*(1–2), pp.41–54.

112. Jia, X., Zhong, X., Ye, M., Liu, W. and Huang, W., 2022. Complementary data augmentation for cloth-changing person re-identification. *IEEE Transactions on Image Processing, 31*, pp.4227–4239.

113. Johnston, T. and Schembri, A., 2007. *Australian Sign Language (Auslan):an introduction to sign language linguistics*. Cambridge University Press.

114. Jordan, M.I. and Mitchell, T.M., 2015. Machine learning: Trends, perspectives, and prospects. *Science, 349*(6245), pp.255–260.

115. Joze, H.R.V. and Koller, O., 2018. MS-ASL: a large-scale data set and benchmark for understanding American Sign Language. *arXiv preprint* arXiv*:1812.01053*.

116. Kain, C., Koschmieder, C., Matischek-Jauk, M. and Bergner, S., 2024. Mapping the landscape: a scoping review of 21st century skills literature in secondary education. *Teaching and Teacher Education, 151*, p.104739.

117. Mlambo, R. and Matfunjwa, M., 2024. The use of technology to preserve indigenous languages of South Africa. *Literator-Journal of Literary Criticism, Comparative Linguistics and Literary Studies, 45*(1), p.2007.

118. Kelly, J.F., McKinney, E.L. and Swift, O., 2022. Strengthening teacher education to support deaf learners. *International Journal of Inclusive Education, 26*(13), pp.1289–1307.

119. Khoa, P.C., 2012. *Noise robust voice activity detection.* (MSc thesis, Nanyang Technological University).

120. Trejo, M., Canfield, I., Brooks, W.B., Pearlman, A. and Guerrini, C.J., 2021. "A cohort of pirate ships": biomedical citizen scientists' attitudes toward ethical oversight. *Citizen Science: Theory and Practice, 6*(1), p.15.

121. Koller, O., 2020. Quantitative survey of the state of the art in Sign Language recognition. *arXiv preprint* arXiv:2008.09918.

122. Kontsewaya, Y., Antonov, E. and Artamonov, A., 2021. Evaluating the effectiveness of machine learning methods for spam detection. *Procedia Computer Science, 190*, pp.479–486.

123. Kothadiya, D., Bhatt, C., Sapariya, K., Patel, K., Gil-González, A.B. and Corchado, J.M., 2022. DeepSign: sign language detection and recognition using deep learning. *Electronics, 11*(11), p.1780.

124. Mehler, A., Lücking, A. and Dong, T., 2023. Multimodal communication and multimodal computing. *Frontiers in Artificial Intelligence, 6*, p.1234920.

125. Kulmizev, A. and Nivre, J., 2022. Schrödinger's tree—On syntax and neural language models. *Frontiers in Artificial Intelligence, 5*, p.796788.

126. Kumar, M.S., Soundarya, V., Kavitha, S., Keerthika, E.S. and Aswini, E., 2019, February. Credit card fraud detection using random forest algorithm. In: *2019 3rd International Conference on Computing and Communications Technologies (ICCCT)* (pp. 149-153). IEEE.

127. Kuštelega, M., Mekovec, R. and Shareef, A., 2025. Perspective—A PRISMA approach. In: Intelligent Sustainable Systems: Selected Papers of WorldS4 2024, Volume 2. *Lecture Notes in Networks and Systems, 1178*, p.425.

128. Turell, H.A., 2025. *The things they left unsaid: language ideologies and the assessment of Signed Language Interpreters* (Doctoral dissertation, Gallaudet University).

129. Coleman, B., 2023. Human–machine communication, artificial intelligence, and issues of data colonialism. *The SAGE handbook of human-machine communication*, pp.350-356.

130. Kyle, J.G., Kyle, J. and Woll, B., 1988. Sign language: the study of deaf people and their language. Cambridge: Cambridge University Press.

131. Coy, A., Mohammed, P.S. and Skerrit, P., 2024. Inclusive Deaf education enabled by Artificial Intelligence: the path to a solution. *International Journal of Artificial Intelligence in Education*, pp.1-39.

132. Ntoutsi, E., Fafalios, P., Gadiraju, U., Iosifidis, V., Nejdl, W., Vidal, M.E., Ruggieri, S., Turini, F., Papadopoulos, S., Krasanakis, E. and Kompatsiaris, I., 2020. Bias in data-driven artificial intelligence systems—an introductory survey. *Wiley Interdisciplinary Reviews: Data Mining and Knowledge Discovery, 10*(3), p.e1356.

133. Leaman, R., Khare, R. and Lu, Z., 2015. Challenges in clinical natural language processing for automated disorder normalization. *Journal of Biomedical Informatics, 57*, pp.28–37.

134. Lederberg, A.R., Schick, B. and Spencer, P.E., 2013. Language and literacy development of deaf and hard-of-hearing children: successes and challenges. *Developmental Psychology, 49*(1), p.15.

135. Leeson, L. and Saeed, J., 2012. Irish Sign Language: a cognitive linguistic perspective. Edinburgh: Edinburgh University Press.

136. Leigh, I.W., Andrews, J.F., Harris, R.L. and Ávila, T.G., 2020. *Deaf culture: exploring eaf communities in the United States*. Plural Publishing.

137. Leigh, I., 1999. Inclusive education and personal development. *Journal of Deaf Studies and Deaf Education, 4*(3), pp.236–245.

138. Tomalin, M., Byrne, B., Concannon, S., Saunders, D. and Ullmann, S., 2021. The practical ethics of bias reduction in machine translation: why domain adaptation is better than data debiasing. *Ethics and Information Technology*, pp.1-15.

139. LeMaster, B. and Monaghan, L., 2004. Variation in sign languages. In: *A companion to linguistic anthropology*. Oxford: Blackwell, pp.141–161.

140. Hosmer Jr, D.W., Lemeshow, S. and Sturdivant, R.X., 2013. *Applied logistic regression.* John Wiley & Sons.

141. Leveson, N., 2015. A systems approach to risk management through leading safety indicators. *Reliability Engineering & System Safety*, *136*, pp.17–34.

142. Li, X., Wang, S., Zeng, S., Wu, Y. and Yang, Y., 2024. A survey on LLM-based multi-agent systems: Workflow, infrastructure, and challenges. *Vicinagearth*, *1*(1), p.9.

143. Liang, Z., Li, H. and Chai, J., 2023. Sign Language translation: A survey of approaches and techniques. *Electronics*, *12*(12), p.2678.

144. Liddell, S.K., 2003. *Grammar, gesture, and meaning in American Sign Language*. Cambridge: Cambridge University Press.

145. Barnes, C. and Mercer, G. eds., 1997. *Doing disability research.* Leeds: Disability Press.

146. Ligeza, A., 2006. *Logical foundations for rule-based systems*. Vol. 11. Heidelberg: Springer.

147. Liu, C., et al., 2015. Financial fraud detection model: based on random forest. *International Journal of Economics and Finance*, *7*(7), p.178.

148. Liu, F., Wang, H., Gong, J., Yi, R., Zhou, Q., Lu, X., Lu, J. and Ma, L., 2024. Emphasizing semantic consistency of salient posture for speech-driven gesture generation. In: *Proceedings of the 32nd ACM International Conference on Multimedia*, pp.7027–7035.

149. Liwicki, S. and Everingham, M., 2009, June. Automatic recognition of fingerspelled words in British Sign Language. In: *2009 IEEE computer society conference on computer vision and pattern recognition workshops* (pp. 50-57). IEEE.

150. Loth, C.R., Kotzé, G. and de Lange, J., 2021. Finding place names: improving the digital documentation and accessibility of SASL place names. In: *Standardisation and the wealth of place names: aspects of a delicate relationship*, p.147.

151. Lu, P. and Huenerfauth, M., 2011. Data-driven synthesis of spatially inflected verbs for American Sign Language animation. *ACM Transactions on Accessible Computing (TACCESS)*, *4*(1), pp.1-29.

152. Magongwa, L.M., 2024. Factors Inhibiting the implementation of a South African Sign Language curriculum in schools for deaf learners. *Per Linguam: a Journal of Language Learning= Per Linguam: Tydskrif vir Taalaanleer*, *40*(2), pp.1-23.

153. Mak, S. and Thomas, A., 2022. An introduction to scoping reviews. *Journal of Graduate Medical Education*, *14*(5), pp.561–564.

154. Manoharan, G., Dharmaraj, A., Sheela, S.C., Naidu, K., Chavva, M. and Chaudhary, J.K., 2024, May. Machine learning-based real-time fraud detection in financial transactions. In: *2024 International Conference on Advances in Computing, Communication and Applied Informatics (ACCAI)* (pp. 1-6). IEEE.

155. Marivate, V., Mots' Oehli, M., Wagnerinst, V., Lastrucci, R. and Dzingirai, I., 2023. Puoberta: training and evaluation of a curated language model for Setswana. In: *Southern African Conference for Artificial Intelligence Research*, pp.253–266. Cham: Springer Nature Switzerland.

156. Marschark, M., Tang, G. and Knoors, H. eds., 2014. *Bilingualism and bilingual deaf education.* Oxford: Oxford University Press.

157. Maryadi, E., Syahrul, S., Maulidya, D., Risnandar, R., Prakasa, E. and Andriana, D., 2022. Hand skeleton graph feature for Indonesian Sign Language (BISINDO) recognition based on computer vision. In: *Proceedings of the 2022 International Conference on Computer, Control, Informatics and Its Applications*, pp.256–260.

158. Mateo, J., Rius-Peris, J.M., Maraña-Pérez, A.I., Valiente-Armero, A. and Torres, A.M., 2021. Extreme gradient boosting machine learning method for predicting medical treatment in patients with acute bronchiolitis. *Biocybernetics and Biomedical Engineering, 41*(2), pp.792-801.

159. Mattos, S.M., Cestari, V.R.F. and Moreira, T.M.M., 2023. Scoping protocol review: PRISMA-ScR guide refinement. *Revista de Enfermagem UFPI, 12*(1).

160. Vohra, N., Chari, V., Mathur, P., Sudarshan, P., Verma, N., Mathur, N., Thakur, P., Chopra, T., Srivastava, Y., Gupta, S. and Dasmahapatra, V., 2015. Inclusive workplaces: lessons from theory and practice. *Vikalpa, 40*(3), pp.324-362.

161. Marshall, M.M., Carrano, A.L. and Dannels, W.A., 2016. Adapting experiential learning to develop problem-solving skills in deaf and hard-of-hearing engineering students. *Journal of Deaf Studies and Deaf Education, 21*(4), pp.403-415.

162. Wang, J. and Napier, J., 2015. Directionality in signed language interpreting. *Meta, 60*(3), pp.518-541.

163. McRoy, S.W., Channarukul, S. and Ali, S.S., 2003. An augmented template-based approach to text realization. *Natural Language Engineering, 9*(4), pp.381–420.

164. Meiklejohn, C., Westaway, L., Westaway, A.F. and Long, K.A., 2021. A review of South African primary school literacy interventions from 2005 to 2020. *South African Journal of Childhood Education, 11*(1), pp.1–11.

165. Sutton-Spence, R., 2008. Mouthings and simultaneity in British sign language. In: *Simultaneity in signed languages: form and function* (pp. 147-162). John Benjamins Publishing Company.s

166. Miller, K., 2024. Accessibility of substance use disorder services for the d/Deaf and Hard of Hearing Community.

167. Millett, P., 2021. Accuracy of speech-to-text captioning for students who are Deaf or hard of hearing. *Journal of Educational, Pediatric & (Re) Habilitative Audiology, 25.*

168. Sandler, W., Gullberg, M. and Padden, C., 2019. Visual language. *Frontiers in Psychology, 10*, p.1765.

169. Moape, T., Muzambi, A. and Chimbo, B., 2025. Evaluating the impact of deep learning model architecture on sign language recognition accuracy in low-resource context. *The Indonesian Journal of Computer Science, 14*(1).

170. Mogofe, R.A. and Athiemoolam, L., 2025. The effects of case study teaching on learners' language literacy skills in physical sciences classrooms. *International Journal of Educational Innovation and Research*, *4*(1), pp.144–155.

171. Mojapelo, S.M., 2023. Whopping low reading literacies in South Africa. *South African Journal of Libraries and Information Science*, *89*(1), pp.1–14.

172. Kohnke, S. and Zaugg, T., 2025. Artificial Intelligence: an untapped opportunity for equity and access in STEM education. *Education Sciences*, *15*(1), p.68.sss

173. Morgan, R., ed., 2008. *Deaf me normal: Deaf South Africans tell their life stories*. Pretoria: Unisa Press.

174. Morgan, R. and Kaneko, M., 2017. Being and belonging as Deaf South Africans: Multiple identities in SASL poetry. *African Studies*, *76*(3), pp.320-336.

175. Murray, J.J., 2015. Language planning and sign language rights. *Sign Language Studies*, *15*(4), pp.375-378.

176. Moryossef, A., 2024. Real-time multilingual Sign Language processing. *arXiv preprint* arXiv:2412.01991.

177. Moryossef, A., Müller, M., Göhring, A., Jiang, Z., Goldberg, Y. and Ebling, S., 2023. An open-source gloss-based baseline for spoken to signed language translation. In: *Proceedings of the Second International Workshop on Automatic Translation for Signed and Spoken Languages*, pp.22–33.

178. Motlhabi, M.B., Glaser, M. and Tucker, W.D., 2013. SignSupport: A limited communication domain mobile aid for a Deaf patient at the pharmacy.

179. Mucherino, A., Papajorgji, P.J. and Pardalos, P.M., 2009. k-Nearest neighbor classification. In: *Data mining in agriculture*. New York: Springer (Springer Optimization and Its Applications), pp.83–106.

180. Grenoble, L.A. and Singerman, A.R., 2014. *Minority languages* (pp. 9780199772810-0176). Oxford: Oxford University Press.

181. Mukhopadhyay, T., Rajiv, S. and Srinivasan, K., 1997. Information technology impact on process output and quality. *Management Science*, *43(*12), pp.1645–1659.

182. Fontana, S., 2008. Mouth actions as gesture in sign language. *Gesture*, *8*(1), pp.104-123.

183. Munn, Z., Peters, M.D., Stern, C., Tufanaru, C., McArthur, A. and Aromataris, E., 2018. Systematic review or scoping review? Guidance for authors when choosing between a systematic or scoping review approach. *BMC Medical Research Methodology*, *18*, pp.1–7.

184. Murphy, K., Di Ruggiero, E., Upshur, R., Willison, D.J., Malhotra, N., Cai, J.C., Malhotra, N., Lui, V. and Gibson, J., 2021. Artificial intelligence for good health: a scoping review of the ethics literature. *BMC Medical Ethics*, *22*, pp.1–17.

185. Bragg, D., Caselli, N., Hochgesang, J.A., Huenerfauth, M., Katz-Hernandez, L., Koller, O., Kushalnagar, R., Vogler, C. and Ladner, R.E., 2021. The fate landscape of sign language AIdatasets: an interdisciplinary perspective. *ACM Transactions on Accessible Computing (TACCESS)*, *14*(2), pp.1-45.

186. McLester-Davis, L.W., Gleason, C.E., Blazel, H.M., Zuelsdorff, M., Lambrou, N.H. and Parker, T., 2023. Indigenous data sovereignty in the context of big data. *Alzheimer's & Dementia, 19*, p.e068387.

187. Nalepa, G.J. and Bobek, S., 2014. Rule-based solution for context-aware reasoning on mobile devices. *Computer Science and Information Systems, 11*(1), pp.171–193.

188. Napier, J. and Leeson, L., 2016. *Sign language in action.* Basingstoke: Palgrave Macmillan.

189. Naranjo-Zeledón, L., Peral, J., Ferrández, A. and Chacón-Rivas, M., 2019. A systematic mapping of translation-enabling technologies for sign languages. *Electronics, 8*(9), p.1047.

190. Natarajan, B. and Elakkiya, R., 2022. Dynamic GAN for high-quality sign language video generation from skeletal poses using generative adversarial networks. *Soft Computing, 26*(23), pp.13153–13175.

191. Okorie, C. and Marivate, V., 2024. Copyright, innovation, and local access in African NLP. *Carnegie Endowment for International Peace* https://carnegieendowment.org/research /2024/04/how-african- nlp-experts-are-navigating-the-challenges-of-copyright-innovation-and-access.

192. Mashwama, X.N. and Madubela, B., 2024, December. A systematic review of academic exclusion in higher education institutions in South Africa: causes, consequences, and remedial measures. In: *The Focus Conference (TFC 2024)* (pp. 30-59). Atlantis Press.

193. Hechler, E., Oberhofer, M., Schaeck, T., Hechler, E., Oberhofer, M. and Schaeck, T., 2020. AI and governance. *Deploying AI in the enterprise: IT approaches for design, DevOps, governance, change management, blockchain, and quantum computing*, pp.165-211.

194. Zwitserlood, I., Van Gijn, I., Ackema, P., Brandt, P. and Schoorlemmer, M., 2006. Agreement phenomena in Sign Language of the Netherlands. *Arguments and agreement*, pp.195-229.

195. Ouyang, H., Ma, X. and Wu, X., 2022. The prevalence and determinants of COVID-19 vaccine hesitancy in the age of infodemic. *Human Vaccines & Immunotherapeutics, 18*(1), p.2013694.

196. Oza, N.C. and Tumer, K., 2008. Classifier ensembles: select real-world applications. *Information Fusion, 9*(1), pp.4–20.

197. Kurniawati, R.D., Wijiastuti, A. and Yuliyati, Y., 2021. Science learning development for the deaf: a digital literacy-based learning design. *Jurnal Inovasi Pendidikan IPA, 7*(2), pp.182-194.

198. Parmar, A., Katariya, R. and Patel, V., 2018, August. A review on random forest: an ensemble classifier. In: *International Conference on Intelligent Data Communication Technologies and Internet of Things* (pp. 758-763). Cham: Springer International Publishing.

199. Reagan, T., 2008. South African Sign Language and language-in-education policy in South Africa. *Stellenbosch Papers in Linguistics, 38*(1), pp.165-190.

200. Ellis-Robinson, T., 2021. Identity development and intersections of disability, race, and STEM: illuminating perspectives on equity. *Cultural Studies of Science Education, 16*(4), pp.1149-1162.

201. Pfau, R., Steinbach, M. and Woll, B., eds., 2012. *Sign Language: an international handbook.* Berlin: De Gruyter Mouton.

202. Pigou, L., Dieleman, S., Kindermans, P.J. and Schrauwen, B., 2015. Sign language recognition using convolutional neural networks. In: *Computer Vision-ECCV 2014 Workshops: Zurich, Switzerland, September 6-7 and 12, 2014, Proceedings, Part I 13* (pp. 572-578). Springer International Publishing.

203. Mokofe, W.M., 2023. Digital transformations of the South African legal landscape. *Journal of Digital Technologies and Law, 1*(4), pp.1087-1104.

204. Pisner, D.A. and Schnyer, D.M., 2020. Support vector machine. In: *Machine learning.* Amsterdam: Elsevier, pp.101–121.

205. Pollock, D., Tricco, A.C., Peters, M.D., Mclnerney, P.A., Khalil, H., Godfrey, C.M., Alexander, L.A. and Munn, Z., 2022. Methodological quality, guidance, and tools in scoping reviews: a scoping review protocol. *JBI Evidence Synthesis, 20*(4), pp.1098–1105.

206. Pool, J., Fatehi, F. and Akhlaghpour, S., 2021. Infodemic, misinformation and disinformation in pandemics: Scientific landscape and the road ahead for public health informatics research. In: *Public Health and Informatics.* Amsterdam: IOS Press, pp.764–768.

207. Prabhudesai, M., Tung, H.Y.F., Javed, S.A., Sieb, M., Harley, A.W. and Fragkiadaki, K., 2020. Embodied language grounding with 3D visual feature representations. In: *Proceedings of the IEEE/CVF Conference on Computer Vision and Pattern Recognition*, pp.2220–2229.

208. Prinsloo, B.A., 2003. An introductory South African Sign Language (SASL) grammar for the beginner sign language student. *University of the Free State.*

209. Prokott, K.E., Tamura, H. and Fleming, R.W., 2021. Gloss perception: searching for a deep neural network that behaves like humans. *Journal of Vision, 21*(12), pp.14–14.

210. Fasold, R. and Connor-Linton, J., 2006. *An introduction to language and linguistics.* Cambridge university press.

211. Rahman, S., Pal, S., Mittal, S., Chawla, T. and Karmakar, C., 2024. SYN-GAN: A robust intrusion detection system using GAN-based synthetic data for IoT security. *Internet of Things, 26*, p.101212.

212. Raina, R., Madhavan, A. and Ng, A.Y., 2009, June. Large-scale deep unsupervised learning using graphics processors. In: *Icml* (Vol. 9, pp. 873-880).

213. Rastgoo, R., Kiani, K., Escalera, S. and Sabokrou, M., 2021. Sign language production: a review. In: *Proceedings of the IEEE/CVF Conference on Computer Vision and Pattern Recognition*, pp.3451–3461.

214. Rathkey, E.S., 2019. *Can ASL-gloss be used as an instructional tool to teach written English to the Deaf?Digital Commons.*

215. Reagan, T., 2006. Language policy and sign languages. *An introduction to language policy. theory and method*, pp.329-345.

216. Reagan, T., 2020. A twelfth official language? The constitutional future of South African Sign Language. *Southern African Linguistics and Applied Language Studies, 38*(1), pp.73–85.

217. Rincy, T.N. and Gupta, R., 2020. Ensemble learning techniques and its efficiency in machine learning: a survey. In: *2nd International Conference on Data, Engineering and Applications (IDEA)*. Bhopal, India: IEEE, pp.1–6.

218. Rish, I., 2001. An empirical study of the Naïve Bayes classifier. *IJCAI 2001 Workshop on Empirical Methods in Artificial Intelligence*, 3.

219. Paludneviciene, R., Hauser, P.C., Daggett, D.J. and Kurz, K.B., 2012. Issues and trends in sign language assessment. *Assessing literacy in deaf individuals: neurocognitive measurement and predictors*, pp.191-207.

220. Roy, S.S. and Viswanatham, V.M., 2016. Classifying spam emails using artificial intelligent techniques. *International Journal of Engineering Research in Africa, 22*, pp.152–161.

221. Leavy, S., O'Sullivan, B. and Siapera, E., 2020. Data, power and bias in artificial intelligence. *arXiv preprint arXiv:2008.07341*.

222. Schmidhuber, J., 2014. Deep learning in neural networks: an overview. *Neural Networks*, *61*, pp.85–117.

223. Selçuk, A.A., 2019. A guide for systematic reviews: PRISMA. *Turkish Archives of Otorhinolaryngology*, *57*(1), pp.57.

224. Sen, P.C., Hajra, M. and Ghosh, M., 2020. Supervised classification algorithms in machine learning: A survey and review. In: Mandal, J.K. and Bhattacharya, D., eds. *Emerging technology in modelling and graphics*. Singapore: Springer (Advances in Intelligent Systems and Computing), pp.99–111.

225. McBride, E., Peters, E.S. and Judd, S., 2021, March. Design considerations for inclusive AI curriculum materials. In: *Proceedings of the 52nd ACM Technical sSmposium on Computer Science Education* (pp. 1370-1370).

226. Bragg, D., Koller, O., Caselli, N. and Thies, W., 2020, October. Exploring collection of sign language datasets: Privacy, participation, and model performance. In: *Proceedings of the 22nd International ACM SIGACCESS Conference on Computers and Accessibility* (pp. 1-14).

227. Shyam, R. et al., 2020. Competitive analysis of the top gradient boosting machine learning algorithms. In: *2020 2nd International Conference on Advances in Computing, Communication Control and Networking (ICACCCN)*. Greater Noida, India: IEEE, pp.191–196.

228. Silver, H., 2007. The process of social exclusion: The dynamics of an evolving concept. *Chronic Poverty Research Centre Working Paper*, (95).

229. Simonyan, K. and Zisserman, A., 2014. Very deep convolutional networks for large-scale image recognition. *arXiv preprint arXiv:1409.1556*.

230. Fontana, M. and Mitra, S., 2023. Inclusive trade and persons with disabilities. *Ministry of Foreign Affairs in Finland*. pp.1-99.

231. Siyavoshi, S. and Sibanda, P., 2024. Urban toponymy in South African Sign Language (SASL): Patterns and variations. *Sign Language Studies*, *24*(4), pp.942–960.

232. Datta, R., 2018. Decolonizing both researcher and research and its effectiveness in Indigenous research. *Research Ethics*, *14*(2), pp.1-24.

233. Southwood, F., White, M.J., Brookes, H., Pascoe, M., Ndhambi, M., Yalala, S., Mahura, O., Mössmer, M., Oosthuizen, H., Brink, N. and Alcock, K., 2021. Sociocultural factors affecting vocabulary development in young South African children. *Frontiers in Psychology*, *12*, p.642315.

234. Spelmen, V.S. and Porkodi, R., 2018, March. A review on handling imbalanced data. In: *2018 International Conference on Current Trends towards Converging Technologies (ICCTCT)* (pp. 1-11). IEEE.

235. Stam, R. and Shohat, E., 1994. Contested histories: Eurocentrism, multiculturalism, and the media. In: *Multiculturalism: a critical reader*, pp.296–324.

236. Starner, T., 1995. *Visual recognition of American sign language using hidden Markov models* (Doctoral dissertation, Massachusetts Institute of Technology).

237. Stone, C., 2009. *Towards a Deaf translation norm*. Washington, D.C.: Gallaudet University Press.s

238. Soylu, D. and Şahin, A., 2024. The Role of AI in Supporting Indigenous Languages. *Sciences*, *2*(4), pp.11-18.

239. Sultana, J. and Jilani, A.K., 2018. Predicting breast cancer using logistic regression and multi-class classifiers. *International Journal of Engineering & Technology*, *7*(4.20), pp.22-26.

240. Sutton, V., 1990. *Lessons in SignWriting: textbook and workbook*. La Jolla, CA: Deaf Action Committee for SignWriting.

241. Sutton, V. and Frost, R., 2008. *SignWriting: the world's first writing system for sign languages*. La Jolla, CA: Center for Sutton Movement Writing.

242. Sutton-Spence, R., & Woll, B. (1999). *The Linguistics of British Sign Language: an introduction*. Cambridge University Press.

243. Talmy, L., 2003. The representation of spatial structure in spoken and signed language. In: *Perspectives on classifier constructions in sign languages* (pp. 179-206). Psychology Press.

244. Tan, S., Gong, B., Wang, X., Zhang, S., Zheng, D., Zheng, R., Zheng, K., Chen, J. and Yang, M., 2024. Animate-x: universal character image animation with enhanced motion representation. *arXiv preprint arXiv:2410.10306*.

245. Tangcharoensathien, V., Calleja, N., Nguyen, T., et al. (2021). Framework for managing the COVID-19 infodemic: methods and results of an online, crowdsourced WHO technical consultation. *Journal of Medical Internet Research*, *23*(2), e23258.

246. Taylor, N.. and Mawoyo, M.., 2022. Professionalising teaching: the case of language and literacy. *Early grade reading in South Africa*, pp.164-178.

247. Teodoro, D., Ferdowsi, S., Borissov, N., Kashani, E., Vicente Alvarez, D., Copara, J., Gouareb, R., Naderi, N. and Amini, P., 2021. Information retrieval in an infodemic: the case of COVID-19 publications. *Journal of medical Internet research*, *23*(9), p.e30161.

248. Thangaraj, H., Chenat, A., Walia, J.S. and Marivate, V., 2024. Cross-lingual transfer of multilingual models on low resource African Languages. *arXiv preprint arXiv:2409.10965.*

249. Thomsen, K., Christensen, A.L., Iversen, L., Lomholt, H.B. and Winther, O., 2020. Deep learning for diagnostic binary classification of multiple-lesion skin diseases. *Frontiers in medicine*, *7*, p.574329.

250. Tovide, A.S., Tucker, W.D. and Ajayi, O.O., 2022, May. Signsupport: an emergency mobile application for the Deaf. In: *2022 IST-Africa Conference (IST-Africa)* (pp. 1-13). IEEE.

251. Trabucchi, D. and Buganza, T., 2019. Data-driven innovation: switching the perspective on big data. *European Journal of Innovation Management*, *22*(1), pp.23-40.

252. Tricco, A.C., Lillie, E., Zarin, W., O'brien, K., Colquhoun, H., Kastner, M., Levac, D., Ng, C., Sharpe, J.P., Wilson, K. and Kenny, M., 2016. A scoping review on the conduct and reporting of scoping reviews. *BMC medical research methodology*, *16*, pp.1-10.

253. Tricco, A.C., Lillie, E., Zarin, W., O'Brien, K.K., Colquhoun, H., Levac, D., Moher, D., Peters, M.D., Horsley, T., Weeks, L. and Hempel, S., 2018. PRISMA extension for scoping reviews (PRISMA-ScR): checklist and explanation. *Annals of internal medicine*, *169*(7), pp.467-473.

254. Tucker, W.D., 2015. Beyond traditional ethics when developing assistive technology for and with Deaf people in developing regions. In: *Ethical engineering for international development and environmental sustainability* (pp. 293-323). London: Springer London.

255. Turner, G.H., 2009. Sign language planning: pragmatism, pessimism and principles. *Current Issues in Language Planning*, *10*(3), pp.243-254.

256. Tuveri, F., 2024. A comprehensive review of sign language production. *Journal of Computer-Assisted Linguistic Research*, *8*, pp.1-22.

257. Tyrone, M. (2020). *Phonetics of sign language*. In: *Oxford Research Encyclopedia of Linguistics*. Oxford University Press.

258. Wang, W., Eberhardt, W. and Bromuri, S., 2024. Personalizing communication and segmentation with random forest node embedding. *Expert Systems with Applications*, *255*, p.124621.

259. Sammut, C. and Webb, G.I. eds., 2011. *Encyclopedia of machine learning. Springer Science & Business Media.* Sydney, Australia.

260. Weerakkody, S. and Rajapaksha, S., 2023. Artificial intelligence and mindfulness: systematic literature review based on prisma method. *Journal of Desk Research Review and Analysis*, *1*(2).

261. Wei, Q., 2018, May. Understanding of the naive Bayes classifier in spam filtering. In: *AIP Conference Proceedings* (Vol. 1967, No. 1). AIP Publishing.

262. Weiss, S.M. and Indurkhya, N., 1995. Rule-based machine learning methods for functional prediction. *Journal of Artificial Intelligence Research*, *3*, pp.383-403.

263. Braun, D.C., Gormally, C. and Clark, M.D., 2017. The deaf mentoring survey: a community cultural wealth framework for measuring mentoring effectiveness with underrepresented students. *CBE—Life Sciences Education*, *16*(1), p.ar10.

264. Dunleavy, P. and Margetts, H., 2025. Data science, artificial intelligence and the third wave of digital era governance. *Public Policy and Administration, 40*(2), pp.185-214.

265. Wilcox, S. (2000). *Metaphor in American Sign Language*. Gallaudet University Press.

266. Wolf, T., Trang, S., Weiger, W.H. and Trenz, M., 2024. The technology-behavioral compensation effect: unintended consequences of health technology adoption. *Journal of Information Technology, 39*(3), pp.521-546.

267. Steinbach, M. and Tan, P.N., 2009. kNN: k-nearest neighbors. In: *The top ten algorithms in data mining* (pp. 165-176). Chapman and Hall/CRC.

268. Xu, L. (2024) 'Predictive analysis of customer behavior in retail management based on XGBoost algorithm', in R. Gupta et al., eds. *Recent Advancements in Computational Finance and Business Analytics*. Cham: Springer Nature Switzerland (Learning and Analytics in Intelligent Systems), pp. 295–304.

269. Anderson, R., Wiryana, F., Ariesta, M.C. and Kusuma, G.P., 2017. Sign language recognition application systems for deaf-mute people: a review based on input-process-output. *Procedia computer science, 116*, pp.441-448.

270. Yu, D. and Deng, L., 2016. *Automatic speech recognition* (Vol. 1). Berlin: Springer.

271. Yu, Z., Wilkins, N., Payano, Y. and Kelly, N., 2025. Evaluating an AI Bi-Directional System for Communication between Deaf and Hard of Hearing Individuals and Hearing Persons: A Pilot Case Study.

272. Krishna, S., 2021. Signpose: Sign language animation through 3d pose lifting. In *Proceedings of the IEEE/CVF International Conference on Computer Vision* (pp. 2640-2649).

273. Zhang, H. and Li, D., 2007. Naive Bayes Text Classifier. In: *2007 IEEE International Conference on Granular Computing (GRC 2007). 2007 IEEE International Conference on Granular Computing (GRC 2007).* Fremont, CA, USA: IEEE, pp. 708–708.

274. Zhang, H., Sproat, R., Ng, A.H., Stahlberg, F., Peng, X., Gorman, K. and Roark, B., 2019. Neural models of text normalization for speech applications. *Computational Linguistics, 45*(2), pp.293-337.

275. Zhen, Z. and Yao, Y., 2021. Optimizing deep learning and neural network to explore enterprise technology innovation model. *Neural Computing and Applications, 33*(2), pp.755-771.

276. Zhu, X.J., 2005. Semi-supervised learning literature survey.

277. Combrink, H.M., Marivate, V. and Masikisiki, B., 2023. Technology-enhanced learning, data sharing, and machine learning challenges in South African education. *Education Sciences, 13*(5), p.438.

CONTRIBUTING AUTHORS

Dr. Herkulaas Combrink
CombrinkHM@ufs.ac.za

Dr. Patrick Sibanda
2024947778@ufs.ac.za

Mr. Nick Coetzee
CoetzeeNP@ufs.ac.za

Ms. Charne Bornman
BornmanC@ufs.ac.za

Ms. Gloria Motshoeneng
2017518461@ufs4life.ac.za

Dr. Chrismi-Rinda Loth
LothC@ufs.ac.za

Mrs.Elizabeth Deysel
elizabeth.deysel@gmail.com

Dr. Sara Siyavoshi
2025114899@ufs.ac.za

www.ingramcontent.com/pod-product-compliance
Lightning Source LLC
LaVergne TN
LVHW060042210926
848481LV00013B/3934
* 9 7 8 1 0 6 7 1 5 5 9 2 6 *